1001 Random and Reminiscent Memories of 90s PC Nostalgia

∿

Rediscover Forgotten Computer Terms, for Tech Enthusiasts, Gamers, and Geeks

altara.media

ISBN: 979-8-88-467618-3

Copyright © 2024 by altara.media

ALL RIGHTS RESERVED

No part of this book may be reproduced, stored in a retrieval system, or transmitted in any form or by any means, electronic, mechanical, photocopying, recording, scanning, or otherwise, without the prior written permission of the publisher.

DEDICATION

To the legendary developers of the iconic 90s PC games,

This dedication is a tribute to the visionaries, the night owls, the relentless programmers, artists, designers, and composers who crafted the worlds that defined a generation. In an era of floppy disks, dial-up internet, and burgeoning digital frontiers, you pushed the limits of imagination and technology to create experiences that were more than games—they were gateways to new realities.

Your creativity fuelled our adventures through pixelated landscapes, from the dark corridors of Doom to the sprawling realms of Warcraft. You gave us puzzles that challenged our intellect in Myst, narratives that enriched our understanding of storytelling in Half-Life, and battles that tested our strategies in StarCraft. Through titles like The Sims, you allowed us to play God in the microcosms of virtual lives, while Age of Empires let us rewrite history with the click of a mouse.

But beyond the games themselves, you fostered a sense of community. You inspired us to connect over modems and share strategies, fan fiction, and mods. You showed us the power of collaboration, of shared passion, and of collective imagination.

So, here's to you—the architects of digital dreams. Your work did not just entertain; it inspired, it educated, and it connected us. You laid the foundations for the virtual worlds we inhabit today, and your influence resonates in every corner of the gaming industry.

Thank you for your ingenuity, your perseverance, and your unwavering belief in the potential of pixels. Your legacy is not just in the code you wrote or the pixels you pushed but in the hearts of everyone who ever escaped into the worlds you created.

Here's to the legends of the 90s PC gaming era. Your creations continue to inspire, entertain, and remind us of the magic that happens when imagination meets innovation.

CONTENTS

Introduction	7
Pixelated Adventures: Gaming in the 90s	9
Creative Licensing Models	19
Genre Genesis: Popular Gaming Categories	26
Digital Dream Factories: Iconic Game Studios	34
Beeps and Boops: Hardware Setup	43
Making it work: Machine Config	69
Operating Systems of Yore	75
Floppy to CD: Software Evolution	87
In Print: Computer Magazines	101
TV Shows for the Techie	104
Reel Tech: Movies with 90s Computing	108
Echoes of a Decade: The Quintessential Sounds of 90s PCs	110
The Symphony of Modems: Connecting the 90s	116
The Web We Wove: Early Networking	122
Virtual Frontiers: Websites and Services	128
Pixel Pioneers: Graphics that Defined an Era	139
The BIOS Backstory	144
Plugging In: The Ports of Yesteryear	149
Peripherals of the Past	151
Iconic Tech Brands	155
Expansion Quest: Standards of the 90s	161
Faded Futures: The Tech that Time Forgot	166
Juicy Controversies	173
Final Fact	177

INTRODUCTION

Embark on a journey back in time with "1001 Random and Reminiscent Memories of 90s PC Nostalgia," a meticulously crafted compendium that celebrates an era when technology and imagination collided to create worlds beyond our wildest dreams. This book is a homage to the golden age of 90s PC gaming—a time when the beeps and boops of dial-up internet were the gates to new dimensions, and floppy disks held adventures waiting to be unleashed.

As you flip through these pages, you'll rediscover forgotten gems and the pioneering spirit of developers who dared to dream big. From the clunky charm of the first home PCs to the ground breaking games that defined a generation, this collection serves as a time capsule for tech enthusiasts, gamers, and geeks alike. Whether you're a veteran who lived through these exciting times or a newcomer eager to explore the roots of modern gaming, there's something here for everyone.

This book doesn't just recount facts; it weaves a narrative that captures the essence of the 90s PC gaming scene—its triumphs, challenges, and the indelible mark it left on the fabric of pop culture. It's a story of innovation and creativity, where pixels and code combined to create immersive experiences that captivated millions.

Prepare to delve into the heart of an era where gaming went from a niche hobby to a cultural phenomenon, influencing music, movies, and more. "1001 Random and Reminiscent Memories of 90s PC Nostalgia" invites you on a nostalgic voyage to a time when gaming was not just a pastime but a gateway to uncharted territories. Welcome to a celebration of the legends, the gadgets, and the games that have shaped the landscape of entertainment as we know it. Welcome to the nostalgia of the 90s, rekindled.

PIXELATED ADVENTURES: GAMING IN THE 90S

1. Remember when PC games came in boxes? They were often large and elaborate, designed to stand out on retail shelves. An example of this is the original **"Doom" (1993)** box, which featured striking artwork to attract attention.

2. These boxes often included extensive physical extras, such as detailed manuals, reference cards, and sometimes even cloth maps or novelties. **"Baldur's Gate" (1998)** came with a detailed manual and a paper map of the Sword Coast.

3. Many games from the 90s shipped on multiple floppy disks before the widespread adoption of CDs. **"Monkey Island 2: LeChuck's Revenge" (1991)** is a notable example, initially released on floppy disks requiring disk swapping during play.

4. The transition to CD-ROMs in the mid-90s allowed for games to include multimedia content such as video and high-quality audio, enhancing storytelling and gameplay. **"Myst" (1993)** was one of the first games to take full advantage of CD-ROM technology, offering immersive sound and detailed graphics.

5. Some 90s PC games used manual-based copy protection, requiring players to input specific words or codes found in the game's manual. **"The Secret of Monkey Island" (1990)** asked players to match pirate faces with names and phrases from a code wheel.

6. **"Dial-a-Pirate"** was an anti-piracy wheel used in "The Secret of Monkey Island", where players had to align two disks to match a pirate's face with the correct date of their execution to start the game.

7. Flight simulators like **"Falcon 3.0" (1991)** included thick, detailed manuals not only for gameplay immersion but also as a form of copy protection. Players often had to look up specific information or diagrams to continue past certain points.

8. **"Leisure Suit Larry 5" (1991)** implemented a unique age verification system as a form of anti-piracy, requiring users to answer questions that theoretically only adults would know, although it was more about restricting access based on age rather than preventing copying.

9. PC game manuals in the 90s were often substantial, providing not only game instructions but also backstory and lore to enhance the gaming experience. **"Baldur's Gate" (1998)** included a 160-page manual with detailed game mechanics, character creation guides, and lore.

10. Manuals sometimes doubled as copy protection, with games prompting users to enter a word or code from a specific page, paragraph, or line. **"Wing Commander" (1990)** used this method, asking players for specific words from the manual to proceed.

11. **"Civilization" (1991)** came with a manual so informative and well-written that it was almost as celebrated as the game itself, serving as both an instruction guide and a primer on human history.

12. Game manuals could include keyboard overlays or reference cards, providing quick access to game controls and shortcuts. **"X-Com: UFO Defense" (1994)** included a keyboard overlay that helped players manage the game's complex interface more efficiently.

13. Many PC games in the early 90s were distributed on 3.5-inch floppy disks, requiring players to swap disks during installation and sometimes even during gameplay. **"Indiana Jones and the Fate of Atlantis" (1992)** was released on multiple floppy disks.

14. Floppy disks had limited storage capacity, leading to games being spread across multiple disks. **"Monkey Island 2: LeChuck's Revenge" (1991)** famously came on eleven floppy disks for its extensive graphics and audio.

15. Copy protection schemes on floppy disks often included making the disk unreadable or uncopyable by standard means. Games like **"Dungeon Master" (1987)** employed such protection to deter piracy, although this specific game predates the 90s, it set a precedent for others in the decade.

16. As a nod to their limitations and nostalgia, some modern digital distributions of classic games still mimic the floppy disk experience by splitting the game into multiple "virtual" disks. This is more of an homage than a necessity with today's technology.

17. Cheat codes in 90s PC games often unlocked secret levels, infinite lives, or invincibility, becoming an iconic part of gaming culture. The **"Doom"** series (starting in 1993) popularised the IDDQD code for God mode and IDKFA for all weapons, keys, and armour.

18. Some cheat codes were hidden so well that they became legends, only to be discovered through gaming magazines or word of mouth. **"Age of Empires" (1997)** featured the "BIGDADDY" cheat, spawning a powerful car with a rocket launcher.

19. Developers sometimes included cheat codes as a debugging tool, but they remained in the game as easter eggs for players to discover. **"Warcraft II: Tides of Darkness" (1995)** included cheats like "glittering prizes" for extra resources, intended to help during the game's development and testing.

20. The practice of including cheat codes began to decline towards the late 90s, as online multiplayer games gained popularity and the need for a level playing field became more apparent. However, single-player games from the era

like **"SimCity 2000" (1993)** still featured codes like "imacheat" for extra money, reflecting the era's more relaxed attitude towards game modification for fun.

21. Keygens, or key generators, became popular in the 90s as software and games began requiring a unique key or serial number for installation. They were often created by hackers to bypass this form of copy protection.

22. The use of keygens was not just for piracy; in the 90s, it was also a way for enthusiasts to challenge the encryption methods used by software companies. An example of software frequently targeted was **"Adobe Photoshop"**, though the practice spanned across various software types, not just games.

23. Keygens sometimes came with their own music and graphics, turning the act of generating a serial number into a mini-experience. These "demos" showcased the cracker's skills and were a staple of the keygen scene.

24. In response to the proliferation of keygens, software companies began implementing more sophisticated forms of verification, such as online activation starting in the late 90s. This was a direct countermeasure to the widespread use of keygens for popular games like **"Quake" (1996)** and office software.

25. The culture around keygens and cracking groups contributed to the broader demoscene, where coders, artists, and musicians showcased their talents through elaborate presentations that often accompanied keygens. This scene was not solely about piracy but also about competition and skill demonstration within the community.

Cracking groups played a notorious yet influential role in the software and gaming communities during the 1990s, often competing to be the first to crack and release popular games and software. Here are some of the most renowned groups from that era:

- **Razor 1911:** Founded in 1985, Razor 1911 is one of the oldest cracking groups that was highly active in the 90s. They became famous for cracking numerous high-profile games and were well-respected within the scene for their technical prowess.

- **Fairlight (FLT):** Established in the late 80s, Fairlight was known for its high-quality game cracks and contributions to the demoscene. Their work was often accompanied by impressive intros or demos showcasing their coding and artistic abilities.

- **SKiDROW:** Gaining prominence in the late 90s, SKiDROW specialised in cracking DRM systems of PC games. They were known for their rivalry with other groups and their role in the so-called "crack wars," where groups competed to release their cracks first.

- **The Humble Guys (THG):** Active in the early 90s, THG were known not only for their cracks but also for their humorous and sometimes irreverent NFO files. They were among the pioneers in bringing a distinct personality to the cracking scene.

- **Class (CLS):** Emerging in the mid-90s, Class focused on cracking and releasing PC games. They were known for their efficiency and for often being the first to crack new protection schemes.

These groups contributed to the shaping of the digital underground culture, with their legacy continuing to influence the cracking scene and digital rights discussions to this day. Their activities, while illegal, underscored the ongoing battle between software developers and those seeking to circumvent software protection mechanisms.

26. In the 90s, before the widespread use of hard drives for game saving, many games used password systems to save progress. **"Prince of Persia" (1989)** provided players with a level code upon completion, allowing them to return directly to that level in future sessions.

27. Save game codes often included not just level information but also player stats, inventory items, and other game states. **"Aladdin" (1994)** for DOS used a password system that allowed players to resume their game with the specific progress they had made.

28. These codes were sometimes shared among friends or published in gaming magazines, allowing players to skip directly to difficult levels or see parts of the game they couldn't reach on their own. Magazines like PC Gamer often featured lists of these codes for popular games.

29. The complexity of some save codes led to the creation of dedicated code generators and lists, which were early forms of game hacking and sharing within the gaming community. This practice highlighted the communal aspect of gaming in the 90s, where sharing tips, tricks, and codes was a key part of the experience.

30. As PC gaming evolved and technology improved, the need for save game codes diminished, replaced by the ability to save game states directly to the computer's hard drive. This transition marked the end of an era and the beginning of more sophisticated game save systems.

31. The transition to CD-ROMs in the mid-90s allowed PC games to include much more content, such as full-motion video (FMV), high-quality audio, and complex graphics. **"Myst" (1993)** was one of the first games to take full advantage of CD-ROM technology, offering an immersive experience that was revolutionary at the time.

32. Many games released on CD-ROM included extensive voice acting, which was a novelty at the time. **"The 7th Guest" (1993)**, a puzzle adventure game, was notable for its use of FMV and professional voice acting, enhancing the storytelling and player immersion.

33. The introduction of games on CDs also led to the proliferation of "multimedia" PCs, which came equipped with CD-ROM drives and sound cards to meet the

requirements of these new games. This was a significant shift from the earlier era, where such hardware was considered optional or a luxury.

34. CD-ROM games often came with elaborate installation processes, sometimes requiring players to configure their sound, video, and other system settings manually. **"Wing Commander III: Heart of the Tiger" (1994)** is an example where the installation process was part of the experience, involving multiple discs and setup steps.

35. Many PC games from the 90s included elaborate physical extras, such as detailed maps, cloth maps, and figurines, to enhance the immersive experience. **"Ultima VII: The Black Gate" (1992)** famously included a cloth map of Britannia and other trinkets like a Fellowship medallion.

36. Game manuals were not just instructional; they often contained extensive lore, stories, and artwork related to the game's universe. **"Fallout" (1997)** included a manual styled as a survival guide, adding depth to the game's post-apocalyptic setting.

37. Some games came with "feelies," physical items related to the game that added to its narrative or atmosphere. For example, **"The Elder Scrolls: Arena" (1994)** included a parchment map, giving players a tangible piece of the game world to enhance exploration.

38. Collectible cards, detailed character bios, and other lore-related documents were also common in game boxes, providing background information and deepening the game's story. **"Baldur's Gate" (1998)** included a set of illustrated cards featuring characters from the game, alongside a comprehensive manual and guide.

39. Special edition releases would often feature even more elaborate extras, such as soundtracks, making-of CDs, and art books. **"The 7th Guest" (1993)** special edition included a soundtrack CD, which was a novel inclusion at the time

40. These physical extras not only served as collectibles but also played a role in anti-piracy efforts, as owning the genuine article provided a more complete and authentic experience than could be had with a pirated copy alone.

41. The inclusion of level editors with PC games in the 90s empowered players to create and share their own levels, fostering early online communities around games. **"Doom" (1993)** is a prime example, with its level editor, **DoomEd**, sparking a vast modding community that continues to be active today.

42. **"Warcraft II: Tides of Darkness" (1995)** included a map editor that allowed players to create custom battle maps, leading to the creation of entirely new game modes and strategies. This early use of a level editor helped lay the groundwork for user-generated content in strategy games.

43. Level editors in the 90s varied greatly in complexity, from simple tile-based systems to complex environments requiring programming knowledge. **"Build"** was the level editor for **"Duke Nukem 3D" (1996)**, offering advanced features for the time, such as sector-over-sector (rooms above rooms) which was revolutionary for FPS games.

44. These editors sometimes led to official expansions or sequels based on user-created content. The original **"Half-Life" (1998)**, while at the very end of the 90s and slightly beyond the strict confines of the decade, saw its modding scene, particularly with its level editor, give rise to full-fledged games like **"Counter-Strike" (2000)**.

45. The community around these level editors contributed significantly to the longevity of the games, with new maps and mods being created and shared even decades after the original release. **"Quake" (1996)** and its editor, **QuakeEd**, gave birth to numerous mods and custom

and appreciated by fans for its contribution to the game's eerie atmosphere.

46. **"Doom" (1993)** faced significant controversy for its graphic violence and demonic imagery, sparking debates on the impact of video game content on players, especially after it was linked to the Columbine High School massacre in 1999.

47. **"Mortal Kombat" (1993)**, though primarily known for its console versions, also released on PC and ignited public outcry over its explicit violence and "Fatalities," leading to the formation of the Entertainment Software Rating Board (ESRB) in 1994.

48. **"Carmageddon" (1997)** was controversial for its encouragement of vehicular violence against pedestrians and animals, leading to it being censored or banned in several countries. In some regions, pedestrians were replaced with zombies or robots to lessen the impact.

49. **"Duke Nukem 3D" (1996)** attracted criticism for its portrayal of women and crude humour, reflecting broader concerns about sexism and misogyny in video games during the 90s.

50. **"Grand Theft Auto" (1997)**, while more associated with its later 3D versions, began as a 2D top-down action game on PC and faced backlash for its encouragement of criminal behaviour, setting the stage for controversies that would follow its sequels.

51. This list highlights games that were not just popular in terms of sales but also had a significant impact on the gaming industry and culture. How many of these did you play?

    - **Doom (1993)** - Revolutionised the first-person shooter genre and introduced multiplayer gaming to a broader audience.

- **Myst (1993)** - Became one of the best-selling PC games of the decade, praised for its graphics and puzzle-solving gameplay.

- **The Sims (2000)** - Though right at the edge of the decade, it redefined simulation games with its detailed life simulation and open-ended gameplay.

- **StarCraft (1998)** - Not only popularised real-time strategy games but also became a foundational pillar of eSports, especially in South Korea.

- **Half-Life (1998)** - Advanced storytelling in video games and spawned a franchise that remains influential.

- **Diablo (1996)** - Set a new standard for action RPGs with its fast-paced gameplay and multiplayer features.

- **Warcraft II: Tides of Darkness (1995)** - Helped popularise the real-time strategy genre with its engaging gameplay and multiplayer capabilities.

- **Command & Conquer (1995)** - Another cornerstone of the real-time strategy genre, known for its engaging story and competitive gameplay.

- **Quake (1996)** - Built on Doom's success with improved 3D graphics and online multiplayer, influencing countless shooters to come.

- **Baldur's Gate (1998)** - Revitalised the role-playing game genre with its deep story, character development, and adherence to Dungeons & Dragons rules.

CREATIVE LICENSING MODELS

52. **Shareware** allowed users to try a portion of a game for free and then purchase the full version directly from the developer. **"Doom" (1993)** by id Software is perhaps the most famous example, with the first episode being freely distributable and the remaining episodes available upon purchase.

53. The shareware model was instrumental in the success of many small software companies, enabling them to compete with larger corporations without the need for significant marketing budgets. **"Wolfenstein 3D" (1992)**, also by id Software, is another landmark shareware release that helped popularise the first-person shooter genre.

54. Shareware games often encouraged users to copy and share the free portion with friends, leveraging word-of-mouth for distribution. **"Duke Nukem" (1991)** utilised this approach effectively, significantly boosting its popularity and sales.

55. Many shareware games included a built-in order form that users could fill out and mail in with a check to unlock the full version. **"Commander Keen" (1990-1991)**, developed by id Software, offered a seamless way for players to upgrade from the shareware version to the full game.

56. Shareware disks were commonly found in computer shops, bookstores, and through mail-order catalogues. Magazines often came bundled with CDs or floppy disks containing shareware versions of games, such as **"Jazz Jackrabbit" (1994)**, increasing their reach and accessibility.

57. The shareware model contributed significantly to the culture of PC gaming in the 90s, with communities forming around the exchange and discussion of these games. It not

only helped games gain popularity but also fostered an early form of digital community engagement.

58. **Donationware** is a licensing model where the software is freely given, and users are encouraged to donate to the developers if they find the software useful. **"Rogue" (1980)**, the dungeon crawling game that spawned the roguelike genre, is an early example of donationware. While the original 1980s release pre-dates the 90s, its influence persisted into the decade with many developers adopting the donationware model for their own roguelike games, encouraging donations without a fixed price.

59. The rise of the internet in the 90s significantly facilitated the distribution of donationware, allowing independent game developers to reach a global audience without the need for physical distribution.

60. Donationware models often relied on the goodwill and honesty of the user base, fostering a community-centric approach to software and game development. This model was especially popular among smaller developers or individual creators who lacked the resources for widespread commercial distribution.

61. The use of donationware also allowed for the continuous development and improvement of games, as donations directly supported ongoing updates and enhancements. This was evident in the evolution of games like **"Nethack" (1987)** and other community-supported projects, which saw significant updates over the years thanks to user contributions.

62. Freeware games were completely free for personal use, with no expectation of payment or donations, distinguishing them from shareware, which required payment for full access. **"Cave Story" (2004),** although slightly outside the 90s window, is a classic example of freeware that garnered a massive following, indicative of the freeware movement's longevity.

Creative Licensing Models

63. **"Alien Carnage"** (also known as Halloween Harry), released in 1993, is an example of a game that started as commercial software but was later released as freeware by the developer, Apogee Software, allowing free distribution and play.

64. **Freeware** games often relied on community support for distribution, with players sharing games via floppy disks, email, and early internet download sites. **"Liero" (1998)**, a real-time Worms-like shoot 'em up, became popular in this way, with a strong cult following developed through grassroots sharing.

65. The 90s saw the rise of "freeware developers", individuals or small teams creating games as a hobby or passion project, often leading to innovative or experimental gameplay. **"ZZT" (1991)** by Tim Sweeney, founder of Epic MegaGames (now Epic Games), is a notable example that also included a built-in game editor, encouraging players to create and share their own levels.

66. Freeware games sometimes served as a launching pad for developers, showcasing their skills to secure commercial opportunities or to build a portfolio. **"Spelunky" (2008)**, while post-90s, exemplifies the trajectory from a beloved freeware title to a commercially successful indie game, echoing the aspirations of many 90s freeware developers.

67. **Trialware**, also known as "demo" software, provided users with a limited trial period to use the software before requiring a purchase to continue using it. **"Microsoft Flight Simulator" (1990s versions)** often came as trialware on many PCs, showcasing its features for a limited time or with limited functionality before prompting for a purchase.

68. Some trialware games allowed full access to their content for a short period, after which users needed to buy a license key to unlock the game permanently. **"Quake" (1996)** had a shareware version that acted similarly to

trialware, offering the first episode free and requiring payment to access the rest of the game.

69. Trialware was a way for developers to combat piracy while still allowing potential customers to try before they buy, a crucial marketing tool in the pre-digital distribution era. **"Age of Empires" (1997)** offered a trial version with a limited number of playable civilisations and campaigns, encouraging players to purchase the full game for the complete experience.

70. Unlike shareware, which might limit features or content but not the usage period, trialware typically had a fixed trial period after which the software would cease to function or revert to a very limited functionality mode until a license was purchased.

71. Trialware distribution was facilitated by the burgeoning internet, allowing users to download demos directly from developers' websites or through third-party download sites. This method became increasingly popular towards the late '90s, paving the way for the digital game distribution platforms we see today.

72. **Adware** in the 90s often came bundled with free software or games, offering a no-cost experience in exchange for displaying advertisements to the user. An early example includes **"BonziBuddy"** (though more prominent in the early 2000s), a desktop assistant that displayed ads while purporting to help users navigate the internet.

73. Some game developers partnered with advertisers to include product placements directly within the game as a form of adware. **"Crazy Taxi" (1999)**, though more associated with consoles, featured in-game advertisements for real-life brands like Pizza Hut and KFC, blending advertising with gameplay.

74. Shareware games sometimes transitioned to adware versions, where the game was offered for free as long as users agreed to view advertisements. While more

Creative Licensing Models

prevalent in the following decade, the groundwork for this approach was laid in the late 90s with internet connectivity becoming more common in homes.

75. The rise of internet connectivity towards the late 90s increased the feasibility of adware by allowing ads to be dynamically updated and targeted, though this practice was more rudimentary compared to today's standards.

76. User tolerance for adware varied, with some accepting it as a necessary trade-off for free content, while others sought ways to block or avoid ads, leading to the early development of ad-blocking tools and software.

77. **Crippleware** refers to software or games that are distributed in a deliberately limited or disabled form, requiring the user to pay for full functionality. An example from the 90s is **"WinZip"**, a widely used file compression tool that operated as crippleware by offering a trial period after which a license needed to be purchased to continue using its full capabilities.

78. Many games in the 90s used a similar strategy to shareware but were more restrictive, offering very limited functionality or gameplay that teased the user with what the full version could offer. **"Microsoft Flight Simulator"** in the 90s could be considered a form of crippleware, as demo versions provided just enough features to entice users to purchase the full version.

79. The practice of releasing games as crippleware was a way for developers to combat piracy, as the full game required a purchase and typically a serial number or key to unlock, which was harder to illegally distribute than the game itself. This was seen with many strategy and simulation games of the era, where demo versions might only include a few levels or limited features.

80. Crippleware often frustrated users who expected more from the free versions of the software or games, leading to a search for cracks or keygens that could unlock the full

Creative Licensing Models

versions without payment. This inadvertently fostered a burgeoning online community focused on circumventing software limitations.

81. Despite the negative connotations of the term, crippleware was an effective marketing tool, as it allowed users to experience a portion of the software or game, building interest and potentially leading to a purchase. This model was especially common before the widespread adoption of online payment systems, when users had to mail in checks or order by phone to unlock the full version.

82. **Nagware**, also known as "begware", is software that frequently reminds or nags the user to purchase the full version or register the product. A well-known example from the 90s is **"WinRAR"**, a file archiver utility for Windows, which, after the trial period expired, would start showing a popup reminder to buy a license each time it was used, although users could still use it with full functionality.

83. Some PC games would include nag screens before or after gameplay sessions, urging users to register or buy the full game to remove these interruptions. **"Doom" (1993)** shareware version is an iconic example, which included messages encouraging users to purchase the full version for more levels and features.

84. The effectiveness of nagware was debated, with some users finding the constant reminders annoying enough to either purchase the software or uninstall it, while others simply ignored the nags. This approach to software marketing became less common as online payment systems made purchasing software easier and as alternative monetisation models, like freemium, became popular.

85. Nagware was particularly prevalent in utility software and smaller indie games, where developers needed a way to convert free or trial users into paying customers without the budget for traditional advertising.

86. Despite the annoyance factor, nagware was a crucial part of the software ecosystem in the 90s, helping independent developers sustain their projects and continue developing new products.

GENRE GENESIS: POPULAR GAMING CATEGORIES

87. Point-and-click **adventure games** were at their peak in the 90s, with intricate puzzles, compelling storytelling, and memorable characters. Games like **"Monkey Island 2: LeChuck's Revenge" (1991)** set a high standard for humour, puzzle design, and narrative in the genre.

88. **"Myst" (1993)** revolutionised adventure games with its stunning pre-rendered 3D graphics and immersive, non-linear gameplay, becoming one of the best-selling PC games of the 90s. Its success demonstrated the potential for adventure games to appeal to a broad audience, including non-traditional gamers.

89. The use of **Full Motion Video (FMV)** became a popular, though short-lived, trend in adventure games, aiming to bring a cinematic feel to the gaming experience. **"The 7th Guest" (1993)** was among the first to incorporate FMV, blending puzzle-solving with narrated video sequences.

90. Adventure games of the 90s often featured **complex narratives** that delved into serious themes far beyond what was commonly seen in other video game genres at the time. **"Gabriel Knight: Sins of the Fathers" (1993)** is noted for its deep story, exploring themes of family and destiny intertwined with supernatural elements.

91. The decade also saw the rise of **female protagonists** in adventure games, with titles like **"The Longest Journey" (1999)** featuring strong, relatable female leads, marking a significant step toward greater diversity in video game characters and storytelling.

92. The rise of **real-time strategy (RTS)** games in the 90s was marked by the release of **"Dune II" (1992)** by Westwood Studios, which is widely considered the first modern RTS

game, introducing key gameplay elements like base building, resource management, and direct control of units.

93. Blizzard Entertainment's **"Warcraft: Orcs & Humans" (1994)** further popularised the RTS genre, featuring a compelling fantasy setting, competitive multiplayer, and a balanced mix of resource management and tactical combat, laying the groundwork for the future of competitive gaming.

94. **"Command & Conquer" (1995)**, also developed by Westwood Studios, became a cornerstone of the RTS genre with its near-future military setting, introducing a more narrative-driven approach with its use of full-motion video (FMV) for story sequences.

95. The RTS genre in the 90s was known for fostering an early online multiplayer community, with games like **"StarCraft" (1998)** leading the charge. StarCraft's balanced races and strategic depth made it a staple of competitive gaming and a significant part of the early eSports scene, especially in South Korea.

96. **Map editors and modding tools** became a significant aspect of RTS games, allowing players to create custom maps and scenarios, thus extending the longevity of the games. **"Age of Empires II: The Age of Kings" (1999)**, for example, included a map editor that contributed to its lasting popularity and active player community.

97. **"Total Annihilation" (1997)** broke new ground in the RTS genre with its 3D terrain, which affected gameplay, and its emphasis on large-scale battles involving hundreds of units on the screen at once, setting a precedent for future RTS games to incorporate more complex battle dynamics and strategic depth.

98. The 90s RTS games often included **campaigns with branching storylines**, allowing players' choices to impact the narrative outcome. **"Warcraft II: Tides of Darkness" (1995)** featured separate campaigns for the Orc and

Genre Genesis: Popular Gaming Categories

Human factions, with each mission advancing the storyline, enriching the gameplay experience with a compelling narrative.

99. Resource management and economy building were foundational elements in RTS games of the 90s, requiring players to balance the collection of resources like wood, gold, and food while expanding their bases and armies. **"Age of Empires" (1997)** exemplified this with its historical setting, challenging players to evolve through distinct ages, each unlocking new technologies and units.

100. Although already afforded numerous mentions, **"Doom" (1993)** by id Software set a new standard for the **first person shooter (FPS)** genre with its fast-paced action, multiplayer deathmatches, and modding community support, making it a cultural phenomenon and a template for future shooters.

101. Following the ground breaking success of **"Doom"**, the FPS genre saw an explosion of similar games, often dubbed "Doom clones," such as **"Heretic" (1994)**, **"Hexen: Beyond Heretic" (1995)**, **"Duke Nukem 3D" (1996)**, **"Quake" (1996)**, **"Shadow Warrior" (1997)**, and **"Blood" (1997)**. Each game introduced its own innovations to the formula, ranging from fantasy elements and magical weapons to advanced graphics and narrative depth.

102. **"Wolfenstein 3D" (1992)** is often credited as the game that popularised the **first-person shooter** (FPS) genre, with its simple yet addictive gameplay of navigating through maze-like levels while battling enemies, laying the groundwork for the genre's explosion in popularity.

103. The late 90s saw the FPS genre evolve with more sophisticated narratives and enhanced graphics. **"Half-Life" (1998)** introduced seamless storytelling integrated into the gameplay, without the use of cutscenes, pushing the boundaries of immersive gaming experiences.

104. **Multiplayer capabilities** became a defining feature of FPS games in the 90s, with titles like **"Quake" (1996)** pioneering online multiplayer gaming that would become a staple of the genre, offering various modes like deathmatch and capture the flag.

105. The introduction of **3D graphics acceleration** with games like **"Quake"** significantly improved visual quality and gameplay smoothness, setting new graphical standards for the genre and gaming as a whole.

106. **"Baldur's Gate" (1998)** revitalised the computer **RPG** (cRPG) genre with its deep storytelling, rich character development, and faithful adaptation of Advanced Dungeons & Dragons rules, setting a new benchmark for narrative depth in video games.

107. **"Fallout" (1997)** introduced a post-apocalyptic open world with a unique blend of dark humour and moral complexity, featuring a turn-based combat system and a narrative that adapts to player choices, becoming a cult classic for its unique setting and role-playing freedom.

108. The use of **isometric graphics** in RPGs became popular in the 90s, offering a pseudo-3D view that allowed for detailed environments and tactical gameplay. **"Diablo" (1996)** leveraged this perspective to combine fast-paced action with RPG elements, creating an addictive gameplay loop of monster slaying and loot collecting.

109. **"Planescape: Torment" (1999)** pushed the boundaries of what video game narratives could achieve with its philosophical themes, unconventional setting, and characters, emphasising story and dialogue over combat, which was a departure from the norm in RPGs.

110. **Character customisation and choice** became hallmarks of 90s RPGs, allowing players to craft their own stories within the game world. **"Ultima VII: The Black Gate" (1992)** offered unprecedented freedom in exploration and

interaction with the game world, influencing the development of open-world RPGs.

111. **"Populous" (1989)** by Peter Molyneux is credited with creating the **"god game"** genre, where players wield divine powers to influence the development of a civilisation, paving the way for later 90s titles that expanded on the concept of playing a deity-like role over a game world.

112. **"SimCity 2000" (1993)**, the sequel to the original city-building simulation game, expanded on its predecessor with enhanced graphics, more complex city management options, and the introduction of new features like water and electricity requirements, setting a high standard for future urban planning simulations.

113. **"The Sims" (2000)**, although at the very end of the 90s, revolutionised simulation games by focusing on the daily lives of individual characters rather than city or business management, becoming one of the best-selling PC games of all time due to its innovative gameplay and the depth of its simulation of human behaviour.

114. **"Theme Park" (1994)** allowed players to design and manage their own amusement park, combining business simulation with creative design elements, and introducing a playful approach to the simulation genre with its whimsical graphics and humorous scenarios.

115. **"Dungeon Keeper" (1997)**, also developed by Peter Molyneux, inverted traditional dungeon exploration games by putting the player in the role of the dungeon master, designing dungeons and managing minions to thwart heroes, showcasing the versatility and creative potential of the god game genre.

116. The 90s **MMOs** were notable for their subscription-based models, a novelty at the time, requiring players to pay a monthly fee to access the game, a practice that financed continuous development and content updates.

117. These early MMOs introduced the concept of virtual economies, where players could trade goods and services both in-game and, in some cases, for real-world money, highlighting the potential for virtual worlds to mirror complexities of real-life economic systems.

118. **"Ultima Online" (1997)**, one of the first MMORPGs, paved the way for the genre by creating a vast open world where players could interact, trade, and battle with one another, setting a precedent for community-driven online experiences.

119. **"Meridian 59" (1996)** is often credited as the first 3D massively multiplayer online role-playing game (MMORPG), offering players an immersive online world to explore, complete with player versus player (PvP) combat, a feature that became a staple in later MMOs.

120. **"EverQuest" (1999)** took the MMO genre to new heights with its rich 3D environments, deep gameplay mechanics, and a detailed fantasy world that encouraged cooperative play, raiding, and guild formation, laying the groundwork for the social dynamics of future MMORPGs.

121. **"FIFA International Soccer" (1993)** marked a significant milestone for **sports games** in the 90s, offering an isometric view rather than the top-down perspective common at the time, which allowed for more realistic gameplay and set a new standard for future soccer games.

122. **"NBA Jam" (1993)**, known for its arcade-style basketball gameplay, brought fast-paced, over-the-top action to the PC, featuring two-on-two matches that emphasised fun and accessibility over simulation, popularising the phrase "He's on fire!".

123. **"Need for Speed" (1994)** pioneered the **racing game** genre on PC with its emphasis on realism, detailed car models, and varied environments. It was one of the first games to successfully blend arcade-style racing with realistic vehicle physics and performance.

Genre Genesis: Popular Gaming Categories

124. Sports games in the 90s began to include licensed teams and players, adding a layer of authenticity and allowing fans to play as their favourite teams and athletes. **"Madden NFL" series** capitalised on this trend, offering deep rosters and playbooks that mirrored the real NFL closely.

125. The 90s also saw the advent of multiplayer modes in racing games, with titles like **"Mario Kart 64" (1996)** for consoles influencing PC game development. This encouraged the inclusion of competitive and cooperative play in PC racing titles, enhancing replay value and social interaction.

126. **"Colin McRae Rally" (1998)** set a new benchmark for realism in racing games on the PC, focusing on rally racing with realistic physics, weather effects, and varied terrains, influencing the direction of future racing simulations.

127. **"Microsoft Flight Simulator" (1982)** continued to dominate the **flight sim** genre into the 90s with multiple iterations, each improving on realism, graphics, and the number of airports and aircraft available, making it a staple for aviation enthusiasts.

128. **"Falcon 4.0" (1998)** pushed the boundaries of military flight simulations with its dynamic campaign engine, realistic flight physics, and fully interactive cockpit, offering an unprecedented level of detail and immersion for combat flight sim fans.

129. The introduction of **3D graphics acceleration** in the mid-90s significantly enhanced the visual fidelity of flight sims, allowing games like **"X-Plane" (1995)** and **"Flight Unlimited" (1995)** to offer more realistic terrain and weather effects, improving the overall flying experience.

130. Flight sims in the 90s often came with thick, detailed manuals that were necessary to understand the complex controls and mechanics, reflecting the genre's commitment to realism and depth. **"Jane's Combat Simulations"**

series was renowned for this, providing extensive background information and technical details about the aircraft.

131. The 90s saw the rise of multiplayer in flight sims, enabling pilots to engage in dogfights or cooperative missions over the internet or local networks, a feature that was groundbreaking at the time and added a new dimension to the genre. **"Warbirds" (1998)** was among the first to offer online multiplayer dogfighting, setting the stage for future online flight sim communities.

DIGITAL DREAM FACTORIES: ICONIC GAME STUDIOS

132. **LucasArts**, originally known as Lucasfilm Games, became renowned in the 90s for its innovative and humorous point-and-click adventure games. **"The Secret of Monkey Island" (1990)** and its sequel are iconic examples, celebrated for their witty dialogue, memorable characters, and engaging puzzles.

133. The studio was a pioneer in the use of voice acting and high-quality musical scores in video games, significantly enhancing the narrative depth and immersion of their titles. **"Indiana Jones and the Fate of Atlantis" (1992)** was among the first to offer full voice acting in addition to its compelling story and gameplay.

134. LucasArts also developed the SCUMM (Script Creation Utility for Maniac Mansion) engine, which was used to create many of their adventure games. This engine made it easier for developers to script events and dialogue, allowing for more complex narratives. **"Maniac Mansion: Day of the Tentacle" (1993)** is a prime example of the engine's capabilities.

135. Beyond adventure games, LucasArts was instrumental in expanding the Star Wars universe through a variety of video game genres. **"Star Wars: X-Wing" (1993)** and **"Star Wars: TIE Fighter" (1994)** were ground-breaking space combat simulators that allowed players to experience the thrill of flying iconic Star Wars spacecraft.

136. LucasArts was known for its willingness to experiment with different genres and innovative gameplay mechanics. **"Grim Fandango" (1998)**, for example, combined adventure game elements with a unique art style inspired by Mexican folklore and film noir, showcasing the studio's creative range.

137. As you know by now, **id Software** revolutionised the first-person shooter (FPS) genre with the release of **"Doom" (1993)**. id Software was founded in 1991 by four industry visionaries: John Carmack, John Romero, Tom Hall, and Adrian Carmack, in Mesquite, Texas. Their collaboration and unique blend of talents in programming, design, and art drove the studio to quickly become a leading name in the gaming industry.

138. The studio's culture of innovation and risk-taking, combined with a passion for pushing the boundaries of technology and game design, led to the development of pioneering graphics engines and gameplay mechanics that have influenced countless games and developers across the industry.

139. Before Doom, id Software gained fame with **"Wolfenstein 3D" (1992)**, considered the first true FPS game, which laid the groundwork for the genre with its fast-paced action and 3D graphics, despite the simplistic nature of its 3D environment by today's standards.

140. **"Quake" (1996)** further demonstrated id Software's innovation by introducing fully 3D environments and characters, real-time 3D rendering, and the use of the internet for multiplayer gaming, setting new standards for graphics and gameplay in video games.

141. id Software was also instrumental in the development of game engines, with the **Quake engine** influencing the creation of many other games and genres beyond FPS, thanks to its robustness and the company's decision to license it to other developers.

142. The company had a culture of sharing and openness, famously releasing the source code for the engine of **"Doom"** in 1997, encouraging learning and experimentation among developers and hobbyists, and paving the way for the modding culture that is prevalent in gaming today.

143. **MicroProse**, founded by Sid Meier and Bill Stealey in 1982, became synonymous with the strategy and simulation genres, producing some of the most beloved titles of the 90s. **"Civilization" (1991)**, created by Sid Meier, is hailed as one of the greatest video games of all time, allowing players to guide a civilisation from the Stone Age to the Space Age.

144. The studio was also renowned for its detailed and realistic military simulations. **"F-15 Strike Eagle III" (1992)** and **"Silent Service II" (1990)** offered players immersive experiences in air combat and submarine warfare, respectively, with a focus on realism and technical accuracy.

145. Beyond simulations and strategy, MicroProse ventured into the world of fantasy and adventure games in the 90s. **"Magic: The Gathering" (1997)**, based on the collectible card game, combined strategy, role-playing, and deck-building elements, showcasing the studio's versatility.

146. MicroProse's commitment to creating complex and deep gameplay experiences was evident in their pioneering use of technology and game mechanics, which often included detailed manuals and in-depth tutorials to help players grasp the sophisticated systems at play in their games.

147. The influence of MicroProse's titles extended beyond the 90s, with games like **"Civilization"** spawning a franchise that remains hugely popular today, testament to the studio's legacy in shaping strategy gaming and its enduring impact on the industry.

148. **Bullfrog Productions**, co-founded by Peter Molyneux and Les Edgar in 1987, was known for its innovative approach to game design, blending genres and introducing complex simulation mechanics.

149. **"Syndicate" (1993)**, a ground-breaking title from Bullfrog Productions, blended real-time strategy with tactical combat in a dystopian cyberpunk setting. Players

controlled a team of cybernetically enhanced agents, undertaking missions that ranged from assassination to persuasion, using futuristic weaponry and technology, marking a significant departure from traditional strategy games of the time.

150. **"Magic Carpet" (1994)**, another innovative title from Bullfrog Productions, blended action, strategy, and simulation in a unique 3D world. Players controlled a wizard flying on a magic carpet, casting spells to defeat enemies and reshape the terrain, showcasing Bullfrog's commitment to pushing the boundaries of genre and technology.

151. Bullfrog's games were notable for their quirky humour and distinctive visual style, which became a hallmark of the studio's approach to game development, setting its titles apart in a crowded market.

152. The studio's success and innovative game design led to its acquisition by Electronic Arts in 1995, which allowed Bullfrog to reach a larger audience but eventually led to the departure of key personnel, including Peter Molyneux, and the studio's eventual dissolution in the early 2000s.

153. **Blizzard Entertainment**, originally founded as Silicon & Synapse in 1991, quickly rose to fame in the gaming industry for its compelling storytelling, engaging gameplay, and pioneering online multiplayer experiences. **"Warcraft: Orcs & Humans" (1994)** introduced gamers to the world of Azeroth, setting the stage for one of the most enduring franchises in PC gaming.

154. **"Diablo" (1996)** revolutionised the action RPG genre with its dark fantasy theme, real-time gameplay, and randomised dungeon generation, offering a new level of replayability and fostering a robust online community through Blizzard's Battle.net service, a first-of-its-kind for online gaming.

155. **"StarCraft" (1998)** not only perfected the real-time strategy formula with its balanced races and compelling sci-fi narrative but also became a cornerstone of competitive gaming and eSports, especially in South Korea, where it gained a massive following and professional leagues.

156. Blizzard's early commitment to supporting their games post-launch, through patches, updates, and expansions, helped cultivate a loyal fan base. **"StarCraft: Brood War" (1998)**, an expansion to the original game, is often cited as a model for how to enhance and extend the life of an existing game, becoming almost as beloved as the original.

157. The studio's knack for creating rich, immersive game worlds and compelling lore across its titles helped Blizzard establish a unique brand identity and a transmedia presence, including novels, merchandise, and, eventually, a film adaptation, showcasing the depth and appeal of its game universes beyond the PC gaming sphere.

158. **Westwood Studios** is credited with pioneering the real-time strategy (RTS) genre with the release of **"Dune II" (1992)**. This game introduced many of the conventions seen in later RTS games, such as resource gathering, base building, and direct control of units.

159. The studio's most famous franchise, **"Command & Conquer" (1995)**, expanded on the RTS formula by offering a more immersive narrative through in-game cutscenes and a dual campaign structure, allowing players to experience the story from both the GDI and Nod perspectives.

160. **"Command & Conquer: Red Alert" (1996)**, a spin-off of the original C&C series, was notable for its alternate history storyline involving a time-traveling Albert Einstein. It was praised for its balanced gameplay, distinct factions, and its contribution to the multiplayer component of RTS games.

161. Westwood Studios was also known for its work on RPGs before fully embracing the RTS genre. **"Eye of the Beholder" (1991)** was a successful dungeon crawler series that combined real-time combat with puzzle-solving and exploration, showcasing the studio's versatility.

162. The acquisition of Westwood Studios by Electronic Arts in 1998 marked a significant change in direction for the company, eventually leading to its closure in 2003. However, the legacy of its ground-breaking titles continues to influence the RTS genre and the wider gaming industry.

163. **Looking Glass Studios** was renowned for its deep, immersive games that combined complex storytelling with innovative gameplay mechanics. **"System Shock" (1994)** was a ground-breaking title that introduced players to a rich narrative intertwined with first-person action and RPG elements, set aboard a space station with a rogue AI.

164. The studio's **"Thief: The Dark Project" (1998)** revolutionised the stealth genre by emphasising sneaky, non-confrontational gameplay over direct combat, a significant departure from the action-oriented games of the time. It introduced light and shadow as core gameplay mechanics, influencing countless stealth games thereafter.

165. **"Ultima Underworld: The Stygian Abyss" (1992)**, developed by Blue Sky Productions (later part of Looking Glass Studios), is credited with pioneering immersive sim and first-person RPG genres, featuring a fully realised 3D environment that players could explore in a non-linear fashion, setting the stage for future 3D games.

166. Looking Glass Studios was known for its collaborative culture and for pushing the boundaries of video game design, often leading to the development of games that were ahead of their time in terms of technology and gameplay concepts.

167. Despite critical acclaim and a dedicated fan base, Looking Glass Studios faced financial difficulties, leading to its

closure in 2000. However, the studio's legacy lives on through its influence on modern game design and through former employees who have continued to impact the industry at companies like Irrational Games and Arkane Studios.

168. **Ensemble Studios** was founded in 1995 and quickly rose to fame with the release of **"Age of Empires" (1997)**, a real-time strategy game that combined historical civilisations with expansive gameplay, allowing players to advance through ages, from the Stone Age to the Iron Age, marking a significant evolution in the RTS genre.

169. The studio's success continued with **"Age of Empires II: The Age of Kings" (1999)**, which further refined the formula with enhanced graphics, more civilisations, and new gameplay features, including the introduction of unique units for each civilisation, solidifying its place as one of the most beloved RTS games of all time.

170. Ensemble Studios was known for its attention to historical detail and accuracy, making the "Age of Empires" series not only entertaining but also educational, as players learned about different cultures, technologies, and strategies of historical civilisations.

171. Beyond game development, Ensemble Studios contributed to the growth of the online multiplayer community by supporting online play through the MSN Gaming Zone, allowing "Age of Empires" players to compete against each other from around the world.

172. Despite its success, Ensemble Studios was closed by Microsoft in 2009 after the release of **"Halo Wars,"** a shift that marked the end of an era for fans of the studio's RTS games. However, the legacy of Ensemble Studios lives on through the continued popularity of the "Age of Empires" series and the remastered versions of its classic games.

173. **Valve Corporation** was founded in 1996 by former Microsoft employees Gabe Newell and Mike Harrington,

quickly making its mark on the gaming industry with the release of **"Half-Life" (1998)**. This first-person shooter set a new standard for storytelling in video games, blending gripping narrative and immersive gameplay within a seamless world.

174. **"Half-Life"** not only revolutionised the FPS genre with its narrative-driven gameplay but also introduced the world to its powerful game engine, **GoldSrc**, a modified version of the Quake engine. This engine became the foundation for many other successful games and mods, including **"Counter-Strike"** and **"Team Fortress."**

175. Valve's commitment to supporting the modding community led to the acquisition and official release of **"Counter-Strike"** as a standalone game in 2000. Originally a mod for "Half-Life," it became one of the most popular and influential multiplayer FPS games of all time, showcasing Valve's innovative approach to game development and community engagement.

176. In addition to game development, Valve was instrumental in changing the way games were distributed and played on PCs by launching **Steam** in 2003. Though it began as a platform for updating their own games, Steam would go on to revolutionise digital game distribution, becoming the leading platform for PC gaming.

177. Valve's approach to game design and business, focusing on quality, innovation, and community support, set it apart in the industry and laid the groundwork for its future successes and enduring influence on the world of gaming.

178. **Renegade Software** was established in 1991 by members of the Bitmap Brothers and was known for its role in publishing innovative and genre-defining games during the early 90s. The company focused on supporting independent developers, bringing unique and creative titles to the market.

179. One of Renegade Software's most notable publishing achievements was **"Sensible Soccer" (1992)**, developed by Sensible Software. The game became renowned for its accessible gameplay and fast-paced action, redefining football games with its top-down view and precise control mechanism, making it a classic favourite among fans.

180. **"Cannon Fodder" (1993)**, another game published by Renegade, combined strategy and action in a way that was both humorous and controversial. Its catchy theme song, "War has never been so much fun," and the juxtaposition of its light-hearted presentation with the grim realities of war made it a memorable title of the era.

181. Renegade Software was also known for its collaboration with the Bitmap Brothers, leading to the release of titles like **"Magic Pockets" (1991)** and **"The Chaos Engine" (1993)**, games that stood out for their polished graphics, gameplay mechanics, and distinctive visual style.

182. Despite the competitive landscape of the 90s gaming industry, Renegade Software carved out a niche for itself by focusing on quality over quantity, a strategy that ensured their games left a lasting impact on the gaming community, even after the studio's operations concluded.

BEEPS AND BOOPS: HARDWARE SETUP

183. The **Sound Blaster** series by Creative Labs, first introduced in 1989, became synonymous with high-quality audio for PCs throughout the 90s, significantly enhancing the gaming experience with its superior sound effects and music quality. **Sound Blaster 16 (1992)** was particularly influential, setting a new standard for audio in gaming and multimedia applications.

184. **AdLib**, released in 1987, was the first sound card to gain widespread popularity among PC users, relying on FM synthesis to produce music and sound effects. Although it was eventually overshadowed by Sound Blaster, AdLib set the stage for the importance of sound in computer games.

185. The introduction of **WaveTable synthesis** in sound cards during the mid-90s, such as the **Gravis Ultrasound** and later models of Sound Blaster, marked a significant improvement in the quality of music and sound effects, offering more realistic audio experiences in games and multimedia applications.

186. The rivalry between **Creative's Sound Blaster** series and other manufacturers led to rapid advancements in audio technology, pushing the envelope in terms of what was possible for game soundtracks and sound effects, making sound cards a must-have for serious PC gamers.

187. **MIDI (Musical Instrument Digital Interface)** support in sound cards allowed gamers to connect their computers to external MIDI devices or load MIDI music files, offering an unprecedented level of audio quality and customisation for PC games, with games like **"Doom" (1993)** taking full advantage of this technology for its soundtrack.

188. **Creative Labs' Sound Blaster series** not only revolutionised PC sound cards in the 90s but also popularised the inclusion of bundled PC stereo speakers, which significantly enhanced the audio experience for gaming, music, and multimedia applications. The Sound Blaster 16, for instance, often came with a pair of modest stereo speakers that introduced many users to the concept of high-quality computer audio.

189. **Altec Lansing ACS series**, particularly the ACS48, became a staple on desktops for users seeking superior sound quality. These speakers were known for their clear audio and powerful bass, making them a favourite for PC gamers and multimedia enthusiasts who wanted more immersive sound.

190. The 90s saw the rise of **multimedia kits**, which included a CD-ROM drive, a sound card, and a pair of stereo speakers, marking the transition of the PC into a multimedia entertainment system. These kits were instrumental in driving the PC's adoption as a household entertainment device, capable of playing games, music CDs, and later, DVD movies.

191. **Boston Acoustics BA635**, another iconic set of PC stereo speakers from the late 90s, offered a compelling blend of style, performance, and affordability. Their design and sound quality represented a significant leap over the basic speakers that were commonly bundled with PCs, catering to users who prioritised audio in their computing experience.

192. The adoption of stereo speakers for PCs in the 90s also coincided with the development of virtual surround sound software, allowing two speakers to simulate a surround sound experience. This technology, although in its infancy, added a new dimension to games and movies, pushing the boundaries of PC audio capabilities.

193. The **Motorola Lifestyle 28.8K modem** was a popular choice among PC users in the mid-90s, offering a

significant speed boost over the earlier 14.4K modems. Its reliability and performance made it a favoured option for internet users eager to experience faster web browsing and file downloads before the widespread adoption of 56K technology.

194. **56K modems**, introduced in the late 90s, were the pinnacle of dial-up internet technology, offering the fastest connection speeds of the era. Despite being marketed as capable of 56 kilobits per second, real-world speeds were often lower due to line quality and other factors.

195. The use of modems and dial-up connections required a dedicated phone line to avoid interrupting internet access with incoming calls. This led to the common dilemma of choosing between being online and keeping the line open for telephone calls, epitomised by the phrase "Get off the internet, I need to use the phone!"

196. The **USRobotics Sportster 56K modem** was one of the most popular and reliable modems of the late 90s, known for its high-speed connections and robust performance. It became a staple in homes and offices, enabling faster internet access and file downloads than ever before.

197. **Hayes Accura 56K** modems were well-regarded for their quality and compatibility with a wide range of systems. Hayes was a pioneering company in the modem industry, and the Accura line represented their commitment to providing high-speed dial-up access during the peak of the modem's popularity.

198. **Integrated Services Digital Network (ISDN)** was seen as a significant leap over traditional dial-up modems, offering digital transmission of voice and data over ordinary telephone copper wires. Despite its higher cost, ISDN provided speeds of 64Kbps per channel, with the ability to combine channels for speeds up to 128Kbps, making it a preferred choice for businesses and power users in the 90s seeking faster and more reliable internet connections.

Beeps and Boops: Hardware Setup

199. The **3dfx Voodoo** graphics card, released in 1996, revolutionised PC gaming by enabling hardware-accelerated 3D graphics for the first time, significantly improving the visual quality of games, and leading to the popularity of 3D gaming on PCs.

200. **NVIDIA's RIVA TNT** series, launched in 1998, was among the first to offer 32-bit colour support in games, providing a leap in image quality and setting a new standard for future graphics cards.

201. **ATI's Rage** series, particularly the Rage Pro (also released in 1996), was known for its 2D and 3D acceleration capabilities, competing directly with 3dfx's Voodoo by offering integrated 2D/3D solutions that appealed to both gamers and professionals.

202. The **2X speed CD-ROM drive**, which became a standard in the mid-90s, significantly reduced loading times and improved the overall user experience, helping to accelerate the adoption of CD-ROM technology in PCs and making it a must-have accessory for gamers and multimedia enthusiasts.

203. Encyclopaedia software, such as **Microsoft Encarta**, capitalised on the CD-ROM's capacity to store vast amounts of information, including articles, images, and videos, transforming the way people accessed and consumed educational content.

204. The transition to CD-ROMs also introduced the need for **CD keys** as a form of anti-piracy protection, a practice that became common for PC games and software distributed on CDs, adding an additional layer of security for publishers.

205. The **Sony CDU-33A** drive, one of the first 2X speed CD-ROM drives, became the de-facto standard in the early 90s, known for its reliability and faster data access speeds, making it a popular choice among PC users upgrading

their systems to take advantage of the burgeoning CD-ROM technology.

206. The **Creative Labs Sound Blaster CD-ROM drive**, particularly the 2X model that came bundled with the Sound Blaster sound card, emerged as another de-facto choice for many PC users. This combination not only offered improved audio and data access speeds but also streamlined compatibility and installation, making it a favoured solution for enhancing multimedia and gaming experiences on PCs.

207. The **Panasonic CR-563-B** CD-ROM drive, a 2X speed drive that connected through the proprietary Matsushita interface, was widely recognised for its robust performance and compatibility with a broad range of CD-ROM software and games in the 90s. It often required a sound card like Sound Blaster for interface connection, embodying the era's push towards integrating multimedia capabilities into PCs.

208. The **Sound Blaster CD-ROM drive** was the same as the **Panasonic CR-563-B** drive in many configurations. Creative Labs, the company behind Sound Blaster, often bundled the Panasonic drive with their sound cards to provide a comprehensive audio and data solution.

209. **CD-RW (CD-ReWritable) drives**, introduced in the late 90s, represented a significant technological leap by allowing users to write, erase, and rewrite data on a CD, a feature that was revolutionary for data management and sharing at the time. This capability was a game-changer for both personal and professional use, enabling easy backup and exchange of large files.

210. The introduction of CD-RW technology was marked by high prices for both the drives and the media, making it a premium option initially. Over time, as the technology became more widespread, prices dropped significantly, making CD-RWs more accessible to the average consumer by the end of the 90s.

211. **Yamaha** released one of the first consumer-grade CD-RW drives, leading the way in this technology's adoption. Yamaha's innovation in this area helped to establish CD-RW as a viable and flexible option for data storage, contributing to the gradual decline in the use of floppy disks.

212. The versatility of CD-RW drives, supporting both CD-R (write once) and CD-RW (rewritable) media, made them a staple component in PCs by the late 90s, marking the beginning of the end for magnetic storage media like floppy disks as the primary means of portable storage.

213. In the late 90s, the CD-RW market saw competition between different standards, most notably between **Orange Book Part III standards**, which defined CD-RW technology, and proprietary formats. This competition led to initial compatibility issues between drives and discs, until the industry largely coalesced around the Orange Book standard, ensuring broader compatibility.

214. **CD-RW drive speeds** evolved rapidly throughout the late 90s, with early drives offering 2x write speeds, but by the end of the decade, speeds had increased significantly, with 4x write speeds becoming common and higher speeds like 10x on the horizon, greatly reducing the time required to write or rewrite a CD.

215. **DVD-ROM drives** began to appear in consumer PCs in the late 90s, offering significantly greater storage capacity compared to CD-ROMs—up to 4.7 GB on a single layer disc. This leap in storage capacity enabled the distribution of high-quality video content, complex software suites, and large-scale games on a single disc.

216. The introduction of **DVD technology** was marked by the "DVD format war," with two competing standards: DVD-RAM and DVD+RW/-RW. Despite this initial confusion, DVD-ROM, which focused on read-only capabilities, became the standard for most users, simplifying access to multimedia content and software.

217. **First-generation DVD-ROM drives** were relatively slow, with speeds starting at 1x (1.32 MB/s), but by the end of the 90s, speeds had increased to 2x and higher, improving access times and making DVD-ROMs more practical for everyday use in PCs and entertainment systems.

218. **Zip drives**, introduced by Iomega in 1994, offered a significant leap in portable storage capacity with their initial 100 MB disks, compared to the 1.44 MB offered by traditional floppy disks. This made them an ideal solution for backing up data and transferring large files that were becoming increasingly common.

219. The Zip drive became immensely popular for its ease of use and reliability, quickly becoming a staple in both home and office settings for data storage and transfer. Its popularity was partly due to the drive's ability to connect to PCs via parallel, SCSI, or later USB ports, making it versatile and easy to integrate into existing systems.

220. The Iomega **Jaz drive**, introduced in 1995, offered an unprecedented 1 gigabyte storage capacity for its time, making it an attractive solution for professionals dealing with large files, such as graphic designers and video editors.

221. Despite its high capacity and convenience, the Jaz drive was also known for its relatively high cost, both for the drive itself and the disks, which limited its appeal primarily to business and professional users.

222. The introduction of the **Jaz 2GB Drive** in 1998 doubled the storage capacity, further cementing its status as a leading solution for high-capacity, removable storage, although it faced competition from emerging technologies like CD-RW and DVD.

223. The Iomega **Zip 250 drive**, launched in 1998, was an evolution of the popular Zip 100 drive, offering increased storage capacity while maintaining compatibility with the vast installed base of Zip 100 drives.

224. The Zip 250 drive became popular for its balance of affordability, capacity, and reliability, making it a favoured medium for data backup, file transfer, and additional storage among home users and small businesses.

225. Both the Jaz and Zip drives utilised Iomega's proprietary technology, which, while innovative, eventually faced challenges from cheaper, higher-capacity, and more standardised storage solutions like USB flash drives and external hard drives.

226. Iomega's Jaz and Zip products were among the last highly successful removable storage solutions before the dominance of optical media and solid-state storage, marking the end of an era in personal and professional data storage.

227. Despite their popularity, Zip drives faced competition from CD-R and CD-RW technologies in the late 90s, which offered similar or greater storage capacities at lower costs per disk. This shift marked the beginning of the decline in Zip drive usage as optical media became more prevalent for data storage and sharing.

228. The **"Click of Death"** issue, where Zip drives would emit a clicking sound and fail to read or write disks, became a well-known problem, tarnishing the reputation of Zip drives and leading to significant customer dissatisfaction and numerous returns.

229. **DAT (Digital Audio Tape)** drives, initially developed for digital audio recording, found a second life in the 90s as a popular medium for PC data backup, offering capacities up to 40GB (compressed) by the late 90s. Their reliability and capacity made them a preferred choice for small business and home office users for regular backups.

230. **Iomega Zip drives**, while not tape-based, competed directly with tape backup solutions in the mid to late 90s by offering easier access and management of data with their removable disk system, despite having lower capacities

Beeps and Boops: Hardware Setup

compared to most tape solutions. The convenience of Zip drives made them popular for personal backup and file exchange, challenging the tape backup market.

231. The **Travan** tape technology was another popular choice for PC users, offering a balance between capacity, affordability, and ease of use. With cartridges typically holding 8GB to 20GB, Travan drives became a common sight in small office/home office (SOHO) environments for performing nightly or weekly backups.

232. Tape backup software in the 90s, such as **Seagate Backup Exec** and **Symantec Norton Ghost**, simplified the process of scheduling and managing backups, making tape storage more accessible to average users despite the inherently more complex nature of tape handling compared to disk-based storage solutions.

233. Despite their popularity for backup purposes, tape drives and media were often perceived as slow and cumbersome for data retrieval compared to hard drives and optical media, leading to their decline in popularity as primary backup solutions in the late 90s and early 2000s with the advent of affordable, high-capacity hard drives and later, cloud storage services.

234. **Hard drive** capacity leaps were significant in the 90s, with sizes moving from mere megabytes to gigabytes. In the early 90s, a 40MB hard drive was considered substantial, but by the end of the decade, drives like the **Western Digital Caviar 6.4GB** were on the market, showcasing the rapid advancement in storage technology.

235. Physical size reduction was another hallmark of the era. Early 90s PCs often used 5.25-inch full-height hard drives, but the industry standard quickly moved to the 3.5-inch form factor, which saved space and allowed for the design of more compact and desktop-friendly PCs.

236. Speed improvements were also notable, with RPM (revolutions per minute) increasing to enhance data access

Beeps and Boops: Hardware Setup

speeds. Early 90s hard drives typically spun at 3,600 RPM, but by the late 90s, 7,200 RPM drives like the **Seagate Barracuda** series became common, significantly improving performance.

237. The introduction of **IDE (Integrated Drive Electronics)** and later, **Ultra ATA** interfaces, simplified the installation and integration of hard drives into PCs, making them more accessible to the average user by reducing setup complexities and improving data transfer rates.

238. **SCSI (Small Computer System Interface)** drives, while more expensive and typically used in servers and professional workstations, offered better performance and reliability than their IDE counterparts. Products like the **Quantum Atlas 10k II** exemplified high-end SCSI performance in the late 90s, appealing to power users and businesses with demanding data access needs.

239. **IDE (Integrated Drive Electronics)**, later known as **ATA (Advanced Technology Attachment)**, became the dominant interface for hard drives and optical drives in the 90s, largely due to its simplicity and cost-effectiveness. This standard allowed the drive controller to be integrated into the disk drive itself, simplifying the connection between the drive and the motherboard.

240. The **ATA standard** evolved throughout the 90s, with ATA-1 introduced in 1994 and subsequent versions like **ATA-2 (Fast ATA)** and **ATA-3** adding features like faster data transfer rates and improved error detection. These advancements significantly increased the performance and reliability of PC storage devices.

241. **Ultra ATA (or Ultra DMA)**, introduced with ATA-4 and further developed in later revisions, represented a significant leap in data transfer speeds. By the end of the 90s, standards like **Ultra ATA/66** (introduced with ATA-5) were common, doubling the maximum transfer rate to 66 MB/s compared to its predecessor.

242. The **40-pin connector** used in IDE/ATA became a familiar sight inside PCs, with the ribbon cable connecting drives to the motherboard. Master and slave settings, determined by jumper settings on the drive, allowed two devices to share a single IDE/ATA channel, a configuration staple in many 90s PC builds.

243. Despite the prevalence of IDE/ATA, the late 90s saw the beginning of a shift towards **Serial ATA (SATA)**, which would eventually replace ATA in the 2000s due to its faster data transfer rates, reduced cable size, and improved internal airflow within PC cases.

244. **10BASE-T Ethernet cards** became the standard for network connectivity in the 90s, replacing older coaxial cable (10BASE2) networks. This shift facilitated easier and more reliable connections to emerging local area networks (LANs) and the internet, marking a significant step towards modern networking practices.

245. The introduction of **plug-and-play** network cards in the mid-90s greatly simplified network installations for home users and businesses alike. This technology allowed operating systems like Windows 95 to automatically detect and configure network hardware, reducing the technical knowledge required to get online.

246. **3Com and Intel** were among the leading manufacturers of network cards during the 90s, with products like the 3Com EtherLink and Intel Ethernet Express 10/100 cards being popular choices for their reliability and performance, helping to drive the expansion of networked computing.

247. The rise of home internet access in the late 90s increased the demand for network cards, as dial-up modems alone could not meet the bandwidth needs of the burgeoning web. This led to many PCs being sold with network cards pre-installed, a practice that would become standard in the following years.

248. **ISDN and later DSL modems** for home users often required a dedicated network card for connectivity before the advent of USB modems, illustrating the critical role network cards played in connecting the world to the internet during the 90s.

249. The **Intel 486 series** CPU, introduced in 1989, was the first to include a built-in math coprocessor, significantly enhancing performance for applications requiring complex mathematical calculations. This made the 486 a popular choice for scientific, engineering, and graphic design software in the early 90s.

250. **Overclocking** became a notable trend among PC enthusiasts with the 486 CPUs, as users discovered they could run their processors at higher speeds than rated by the manufacturer. This practice, while risky, could significantly boost performance, marking the early days of PC tuning and customisation.

251. The 486 series saw various iterations, including the **DX, SX, DX2, and DX4** models, with the DX2 and DX4 offering double or triple the clock speed of the bus, effectively boosting the CPU's performance without requiring faster memory or peripherals.

252. **AMD and Cyrix** released their own versions of the 486 CPU, providing competition to Intel and offering consumers more choices. These alternatives were often cheaper and, in some cases, offered better performance, highlighting the competitive nature of the CPU market in the 90s.

253. The **Intel 486DX4** was one of the last and most powerful in the series, running at 100 MHz and demonstrating the limits of what could be achieved with the 486 architecture before the transition to the Pentium series, which offered even greater performance improvements and multimedia capabilities.

254. The **Intel Pentium processor**, launched in 1993, represented a significant leap forward in PC computing,

introducing superscalar architecture that allowed the CPU to execute multiple instructions per clock cycle, significantly improving overall performance for software and games.

255. The Cyrix 6x86's **PR rating system** confused many consumers by suggesting its chips were faster than Intel's at the same clock speed, leading to mixed reception when real-world performance did not always match expectations.

256. Both AMD and Cyrix benefited from **the legal settlement between Intel and the FTC in 1995**, which required Intel to license its x86 architecture to competitors, ensuring continued competition and innovation in the CPU market throughout the 90s and beyond.

257. **AMD's K5 processor**, launched in 1996, was the company's first CPU designed entirely in-house, intended to compete directly with Intel's Pentium processors, marking AMD's ambition to challenge Intel's dominance in the high-performance CPU market.

258. **The Cyrix 6x86 CPU**, introduced in 1996, positioned itself as a competitor to Intel's Pentium line, offering similar or sometimes better performance at a lower price point, appealing to budget-conscious builders and OEMs.

259. **AMD's K6 series**, released in 1997, further escalated the competition with Intel by offering superior performance in some applications compared to the Pentium II, particularly in multimedia tasks, thanks to its innovative 3DNow! technology.

260. **The Cyrix MII processor**, which succeeded the 6x86, aimed to compete with both Intel's Pentium II and AMD's K6-2 processors, but struggled with performance consistency and compatibility issues, limiting its success in the market.

261. The **Pentium brand** became synonymous with personal computing in the 90s, with its name derived from the Greek word for "five," representing the fifth generation of Intel's

x86 microprocessors. The Pentium line was marketed for its enhanced multimedia capabilities, appealing to a broad range of users from gamers to professionals.

262. The **Pentium II**, introduced in 1997, brought several advancements, including the transition to the Slot 1 cartridge design for CPUs. This change facilitated better cooling solutions and easier installation, although it was a departure from the traditional socket-based CPU design.

263. **MMX technology** was introduced with the Pentium line, starting with the Pentium MMX in 1996. This technology enhanced the processor's ability to handle video, audio, and graphical data, marking Intel's focus on improving the multimedia experience on PCs, a critical factor in the rise of digital media consumption.

264. **The AMD Athlon processor**, launched in 1999, marked AMD's entry into the high-performance CPU market, challenging Intel's dominance with its superior speed and performance in both business and gaming applications.

265. **Athlon's initial release** featured a clock speed of up to 700 MHz, which was unprecedented at the time, making it the first-ever processor to break the 1 GHz speed barrier in March 2000, showcasing AMD's engineering prowess.

266. The processor was based on the **K7 architecture**, which represented a significant leap forward from its predecessor, the K6, by incorporating an advanced floating-point unit and a fully pipelined, superscalar design for increased efficiency and performance.

267. The Athlon's **integrated L2 cache**, initially off-die and running at a fraction of the CPU speed, was a key factor in its high performance, setting it apart from many of its competitors.

268. AMD's **3DNow!** technology, introduced with the K6-2 but continued and enhanced in the Athlon, provided enhanced multimedia and gaming performance through SIMD (Single

Instruction, Multiple Data) support, competing directly with Intel's MMX and later SSE technologies.

269. **AMD's marketing campaigns for the Athlon** often highlighted its superiority in 3D graphics and gaming performance, directly targeting the growing market of PC gamers and enthusiasts who were looking for the best bang for their buck.

270. The **AMD Athlon was also notable for its overclocking capabilities**, with many enthusiasts and gamers pushing the processors beyond their rated speeds to achieve even better performance, a practice that AMD unofficially supported by making the Athlon relatively easy to overclock.

271. Competition between AMD's Athlon and Intel's Pentium III (and later Pentium 4) heated up the CPU market, leading to rapid advancements in processor technology and more choices for consumers, ultimately driving down prices and increasing performance across the board.

272. The **Intel Celeron processor**, introduced in 1998, was designed as a lower-cost alternative to Intel's Pentium II, targeting budget-conscious consumers and the growing market for entry-level PCs.

273. **Early Celeron models**, such as the 266 MHz and 300 MHz versions, were criticised for lacking the L2 cache, which resulted in significantly lower performance compared to their Pentium II counterparts, leading to initial scepticism among consumers and reviewers.

274. **The "Covington" Celeron**, the first iteration of the processor, faced particular criticism for its performance shortcomings, but it set the stage for Intel's strategy in the value segment of the CPU market.

275. Intel responded to feedback by releasing the **"Mendocino" Celeron processors**, which included an on-die L2 cache

of 128 KB, dramatically improving performance and making the Celeron a more competitive option for budget PCs.

276. The introduction of the **Celeron A series**, with the Mendocino core, was a turning point for the Celeron brand, offering much better value for money and gaining popularity among budget PC builders and even some enthusiasts due to its overclocking potential.

277. Celeron processors in the '90s used the **Slot 1 interface** initially, similar to the Pentium II, but later versions transitioned to the more compact and cost-effective Socket 370, aligning with Intel's strategy to differentiate its product lines.

278. The Celeron brand's success in the '90s laid the groundwork for its continued presence in Intel's product line up, evolving over the years to include laptop, desktop, and even server variants, always focusing on providing a balance between performance and affordability.

279. The **Intel Xeon processor** was introduced in 1998, marking Intel's entry into the high-end workstation and server market, with the Pentium II Xeon being the first in this new line, offering advanced features tailored for demanding applications.

280. Xeon CPUs in the 90s featured L2 cache sizes significantly larger than those in desktop processors, initially up to 2MB, directly addressing the needs of data-intensive tasks such as large database management and professional-grade simulations.

281. The introduction of the Xeon processor also marked a shift towards **multiprocessing capabilities**, with support for dual-processor configurations right from the start, and later models supporting four or more CPUs for increased parallel processing power.

282. The late '90s Xeon processors laid the groundwork for future developments in server and workstation technology,

283. During the early 90s, **SIMM (Single Inline Memory Module)** RAM was prevalent, typically installed in pairs due to the 32-bit bus width of most systems of the time. PCs commonly came with 4MB or 8MB of RAM, which was considered ample for running the operating systems and applications of the era.

284. The transition to **DIMM (Dual Inline Memory Module)** in the mid-to-late 90s allowed for a wider 64-bit data path, enabling single-module installation and supporting the increased memory demands of advanced applications and multimedia content. This transition marked a significant step forward in PC performance and user experience.

285. **SDRAM (Synchronous Dynamic RAM)**, introduced in the mid-90s, became the standard by the end of the decade, offering higher clock speeds and throughput compared to previous RAM technologies. SDRAM's ability to synchronise with the system's bus speed made it more efficient, leading to smoother multitasking and application performance.

286. The cost of RAM saw dramatic fluctuations throughout the 90s, with prices peaking during shortages and rapidly dropping as manufacturing capabilities improved. These fluctuations were closely watched by PC builders and enthusiasts, as upgrading RAM was one of the most cost-effective ways to improve system performance.

287. **EDO RAM (Extended Data-Out RAM)** was another significant memory technology of the 90s, offering improved performance over the older FPM (Fast Page Mode) RAM by allowing the overlap of certain operations. While it was quickly superseded by SDRAM, EDO RAM represented an important evolutionary step in memory technology.

Beeps and Boops: Hardware Setup

288. The **desktop case**, prevalent in the early 90s, was designed to sit horizontally on a desk with the monitor on top, optimising space usage for the smaller desks and workspaces of the time. This form factor was common among home and office PCs, including models from IBM and Compaq.

289. **Tower cases** gained popularity in the mid-to-late 90s as users demanded more space for additional drives and improved air circulation for cooling. The shift towards tower cases, including mini-tower and full-tower formats, allowed for greater expansion capabilities and became a favourite for gamers and professionals running high-performance applications.

290. The **AT (Advanced Technology) case** and motherboard format was widely used at the start of the 90s but began to be replaced by the **ATX (Advanced Technology Extended) standard** in 1995. ATX introduced improvements like integrated I/O ports on the motherboard and a better internal layout for airflow and component access, influencing PC design for years to come.

291. **Beige** was the dominant colour for PC cases throughout much of the 90s, reflecting a utilitarian design philosophy. The late 90s saw the beginning of a shift towards more varied colours and transparent cases, as users sought to personalise their PCs and manufacturers began to see the aesthetic appeal as a differentiator in a crowded market.

292. The introduction of **built-in case fans** and ventilation slots in the later years of the 90s addressed the increasing heat output from more powerful CPUs and GPUs, marking the beginning of modern thermal management practices in PC design.

293. The beige colour scheme dominated nearly all PC hardware in the 90s, from the computer cases and monitors to keyboards and mice. This uniform colour was seen as professional and unobtrusive, fitting seamlessly into both office environments and homes.

294. **Apple's iMac G3**, introduced in 1998, was a notable departure from the beige trend, offering translucent, colourful cases. This design shift not only set Apple apart from its competitors but also signalled the beginning of the end for the era of beige PC dominance, inspiring other manufacturers to explore more varied designs.

295. The choice of beige was partly practical, as it helped to disguise discoloration from aging and exposure to sunlight, common issues with plastics used in computer manufacturing at the time. However, this practicality also contributed to a lack of differentiation between brands and models, making most PCs of the era visually indistinguishable from one another.

296. The **"beige box"** term became a colloquial descriptor for generic, no-brand PCs that were common in the 90s, emphasising functionality over form. These machines were often assembled from parts by local computer shops or DIY enthusiasts, contributing to the pervasive beige aesthetic.

297. The **multimedia PC (MPC) standard** was introduced in the early 90s, defining a set of hardware requirements that included a CD-ROM drive, sound card, and speakers, aimed at ensuring PCs could handle multimedia content like music, video, and games. This standard marked a shift towards more interactive and engaging computing experiences.

298. **CRT (Cathode Ray Tube) monitors** were the standard throughout the 90s, with their bulky design and heavy weight characterising the desktop computing experience. These monitors could display a range of resolutions but were often set to 800x600 or 1024x768 pixels by the late 90s, balancing readability with performance.

299. **The Sony Trinitron CRT monitors** were renowned for their superior image quality and colour accuracy, featuring a unique aperture grille instead of the traditional shadow

mask, making them favourites among graphic designers and gamers.

300. **Mitsubishi Diamondtron CRTs**, similar to Sony's Trinitron, used an aperture grille to enhance image clarity and colour reproduction, competing closely with Sony in the high-end monitor market.

301. **ViewSonic P Series monitors** were widely recognised for their bright, sharp displays and durability, becoming a staple on many desks of both professionals and home users.

302. **The introduction of the 17-inch CRT monitor** was a significant upgrade from the more common 14 and 15-inch models, offering a much larger viewing area.

303. **Flat screen CRT monitors**, such as the NEC Multisync FP Series, began to appear, reducing the curvature of the screen for less distortion and reflection.

304. **Shadow mask technology** in CRT monitors, utilised by brands like Samsung and LG, involved a metal plate with tiny holes to guide electron beams to the correct phosphor coating on the screen, a contrast to the aperture grille approach.

305. **Refresh rates became a critical consideration for CRT monitors**, with models supporting 85Hz or higher reducing flicker and eye strain, a significant improvement over the 60Hz standard.

306. **Ultra-high resolutions** became achievable on CRT monitors, with models like the Iiyama Vision Master Pro 454 and Sony GDM-FW900 capable of displaying resolutions up to 2048x1536, unmatched by early LCD monitors.

307. **Dot pitch was a key specification for CRT monitors**, with lower values (such as 0.24mm) indicating sharper

images. This spec became a critical comparison point for consumers.

308. **The advent of the 21-inch CRT monitor** represented the pinnacle of desktop display technology before the transition to LCD, offering immersive gaming and detailed graphical workspaces, albeit with considerable desk space requirements and weight.

309. **Multisync technology**, allowing monitors to sync with the varying resolutions and refresh rates of different graphics cards without needing manual adjustment, greatly enhanced user experience and versatility.

310. **Anti-glare coatings** were introduced to reduce the reflection from surrounding light sources, a common issue with the glass screens of CRT monitors, enhancing visibility and reducing eye strain.

311. The move towards **digital controls** for adjusting monitor settings replaced the old analogue dials and knobs, allowing for more precise control over display parameters like brightness, contrast, and geometry.

312. **VGA (Video Graphics Array)** became a universal standard for PC graphics during the early part of the 90s, supporting 640x480 resolution in 16 colours, or 256 colours at lower resolutions. VGA connectors and cables became ubiquitous for connecting monitors to PCs.

313. The introduction of **SVGA (Super VGA)** monitors allowed for resolutions higher than 800x600, providing clearer and more detailed images. This was particularly beneficial for graphic design, gaming, and multimedia applications, pushing the industry towards higher resolution standards.

314. In the late 90s, the first **LCD (Liquid Crystal Display) monitors** began to appear, offering a slimmer profile and lower power consumption compared to CRTs. While expensive and less common than CRTs, LCDs marked the

Beeps and Boops: Hardware Setup

beginning of a significant shift in display technology that would dominate the 2000s.

315. **Early LCD monitors** offered a compact and lightweight alternative to bulky CRTs, but initially suffered from poor viewing angles, limited colour reproduction, and slower response times, making them less ideal for gaming and graphic design.

316. **Dead pixels** became a notable issue with early LCD screens, where certain pixels would not light up or display colours correctly, appearing as permanently black or coloured dots on the screen, detracting from the overall viewing experience.

317. **The industry standard for dead pixels** varied among manufacturers, with some allowing a certain number of dead or stuck pixels before a monitor could be considered defective, leading to consumer frustration and confusion over warranty and return policies.

318. The **turbo button** on 90s PCs was designed to switch the computer's CPU speed between two settings: a higher speed for demanding tasks and a lower speed for compatibility with older software that couldn't run correctly at higher clock rates. This feature was emblematic of the era's transitional technology.

319. Contrary to its name, the turbo button's higher speed setting was actually the computer's normal operating speed; pressing the button to the "turbo off" position slowed the computer down to ensure compatibility with older, speed-sensitive software, such as certain games and applications developed for earlier PCs like the IBM PC or PC XT.

320. Many 90s PC cases included a **digital or analogue display** showing the current CPU speed, which changed when the turbo button was pressed. For instance, the display might show 33 MHz in turbo mode and drop to 8

Beeps and Boops: Hardware Setup

MHz when turbo was deactivated, providing visual feedback of the speed change.

321. The turbo button became largely obsolete by the late 90s as advances in CPU and operating system technology resolved the compatibility issues with older software. The disappearance of the turbo button and speed display from PC cases marked the end of an era in personal computing hardware design.

322. The **RealMagic MPEG decoder board** by Sigma Designs was a pioneering piece of hardware in the early to mid-90s that allowed PCs to play back full-screen, full-motion video at a time when standard computer hardware struggled with video decoding. This made it an essential upgrade for multimedia enthusiasts wanting to watch high-quality video on their PCs.

323. RealMagic's MPEG board was particularly popular for enhancing the playback of video CDs (VCDs) and MPEG files, which were becoming more common due to their compact size and relative ease of distribution compared to analogue video formats. It provided a level of video quality that was previously unattainable on home computers without specialised hardware.

324. Beyond video playback, the **RealMagic MPEG board** was also utilised by some PC games of the era to incorporate high-quality FMV (full-motion video) sequences. Games like **"Wing Commander III: Heart of the Tiger" (1994)** and **"Command & Conquer" (1995)** were notable for their use of FMV, and the RealMagic board significantly improved the playback experience on PCs equipped with it.

325. Installing the RealMagic MPEG board involved opening the PC case and inserting the card into an ISA or PCI slot, reflecting the hands-on nature of PC upgrades during the 90s. This requirement for physical installation made it a more niche product, primarily adopted by tech-savvy users and multimedia enthusiasts.

326. As CPU speeds increased and software-based MPEG decoding became more efficient towards the late 90s, the need for dedicated MPEG decoder boards like RealMagic diminished. This shift marked the beginning of the end for specialised video playback hardware in PCs, as general-purpose processors became capable of handling video decoding tasks.

327. **Creative EAX (Environmental Audio Extensions)** was introduced by Creative Technology in 1998 as a feature of their Sound Blaster sound cards, starting with the Sound Blaster Live! It was designed to enhance the audio environment in video games through advanced reverb and other audio effects, simulating more realistic acoustic environments.

328. EAX technology allowed game developers to create immersive soundscapes that could dynamically react to the player's actions and movements within the game. This capability was a significant advancement in audio technology, contributing to the overall gaming experience by providing a deeper sense of immersion in virtual worlds.

329. One of the first games to utilise EAX technology was **"Unreal" (1998)**, which showcased the potential of environmental audio to enhance the gaming experience. The use of EAX added depth to the game's audio by simulating realistic echoes, occlusions, and other acoustic phenomena, setting a new standard for in-game sound.

330. The adoption of EAX by other popular games of the era, such as **"Half-Life" (1998)** and **"Tomb Raider III" (1998)**, helped to cement its reputation as a must-have feature for gamers seeking the most immersive audio experience. These games demonstrated how EAX could be used to create more engaging and atmospheric sound environments.

331. As EAX evolved, it faced competition from other audio technologies and standards, including Microsoft's DirectSound3D. However, Creative's EAX managed to

maintain its relevance through continuous updates and the release of new Sound Blaster models, keeping it at the forefront of PC gaming audio technology into the early 2000s.

332. **Case Modding** emerged as a hobby among PC enthusiasts seeking to personalise their machines beyond the standard beige box. Early mods included custom paint jobs, window installations to view internal components, and the addition of neon lights or LED fans for aesthetic appeal.

333. **Overclocking** became a popular form of modding, with enthusiasts pushing their CPUs and GPUs beyond factory settings to achieve higher performance. Tools and guides proliferated online, sharing techniques for safely overclocking components like the Intel Pentium and AMD Athlon processors.

334. **Cooling Solutions** saw innovative modifications to manage the additional heat generated by overclocked components. This led to the adoption of aftermarket air coolers, the crafting of homemade water cooling systems, and even experiments with Peltier cooling devices for ultra-low temperatures.

335. **Sound Dampening** mods became necessary as PCs became louder due to additional fans and cooling systems. Modders used materials like foam and rubber to line their cases and reduce noise, prioritising a quiet computing experience.

336. **Custom Cables and Sleeving** were used not only for better cable management inside the case but also as a form of aesthetic expression. Enthusiasts would sleeve their cables with colourful materials and arrange them meticulously to improve airflow and appearance.

337. **Front Panel Modifications** allowed for easier access to ports and added functionality. Modders would install additional USB ports, fan controllers, and even LCD panels to display system information or custom messages.

338. **BIOS Flashing** became a method for unlocking additional features or support for new hardware on motherboards. This risky mod could potentially render a motherboard unusable if done incorrectly but offered significant rewards in terms of customisability and performance enhancements.

339. **"Window Kits"**, which included pre-cut acrylic panels and mounting hardware, became commercially available towards the late 90s, making it easier for enthusiasts to add windows to their PCs without the need for heavy-duty tools.

340. **The Rise of Modding Communities** online forums and websites dedicated to PC modding, like Overclock.net and Modders-Inc, became popular gathering spots for sharing projects, advice, and tutorials. These communities fostered a culture of innovation and collaboration that pushed the boundaries of what was possible in PC customisation.

MAKING IT WORK: MACHINE CONFIG

341. The **640 KB memory limit** was a result of the original architecture of the IBM PC, which allocated the first 640KB of the system's memory for programs and the remaining memory for the operating system and peripherals. This limit became a significant challenge as software and games grew more complex in the 90s.

342. **Bill Gates** is often (mis)quoted as saying, "640K ought to be enough for anybody," reflecting the early expectations for PC memory needs. Despite the debate over the attribution and context of this quote, it has become emblematic of the challenges posed by the 640KB limit.

343. Advanced users and gamers in the 90s frequently used **memory manager software** like QEMM (Quarterdeck Expanded Memory Manager) and Microsoft's HIMEM.SYS to optimise the use of available memory and work around the 640KB barrier, especially for running memory-intensive applications and games.

344. **DOS extenders**, such as DOS/4GW, were developed to allow DOS programs to break the 640KB limit and access extended memory. These extenders were crucial for running advanced graphical games like **"Descent" (1995)**, which required more memory than was available in the conventional memory space.

345. The introduction of **Windows 3.0** and later versions in the early 90s offered a graphical interface and better memory management, partially mitigating the limitations of the 640KB barrier by allowing applications to use extended and expanded memory more efficiently.

346. **EMS (Expanded Memory Specification)** and **XMS (eXtended Memory Specification)** were developed as solutions to surpass the 640KB limit. EMS used a paging technique to swap data in and out of the conventional memory space, while XMS provided applications direct access to memory above 1MB.

347. Many PC users had to edit their **CONFIG.SYS** and **AUTOEXEC.BAT** files manually to load drivers high (using commands like **LOADHIGH** or **LH**) and optimise conventional memory usage to run specific games or applications that required as much of the 640KB as possible for themselves.

348. **"Upper Memory Blocks" (UMBs)** were another technique used to free conventional memory by loading device drivers and TSRs (Terminate and Stay Resident programs) into the upper memory area between 640KB and 1MB, which was reserved for system BIOS and peripherals but often had unused space that could be utilised.

349. The 640KB memory limit became less of an issue with the widespread adoption of **Windows 95** and newer operating systems, which were designed to operate in protected mode, fully utilising the capabilities of Intel's 80286 and later processors, and thus not constrained by the 640KB limit of real mode.

350. Despite the evolution of PC hardware and software beyond these limitations, the challenges of managing and optimising memory within the 640KB constraint remain a fond, if sometimes frustrating, memory for those who experienced PC computing in the early 90s.

351. **AUTOEXEC.BAT** and **CONFIG.SYS** were essential system files in DOS-based PCs, used for configuring the system's environment upon booting. These files allowed users to set system preferences, load drivers, and allocate memory resources.

352. Tweaking **CONFIG.SYS** was crucial for optimising memory usage, especially for demanding games and applications. Commands like **HIMEM.SYS** and **EMM386.EXE** were commonly used to manage extended (XMS) and expanded (EMS) memory, respectively.

353. **AUTOEXEC.BAT** often included lines to set the PATH environment variable, allowing users to launch programs from any directory without having to type the full path. It could also contain commands to automatically start up essential programs or utilities upon booting, such as mouse drivers or network scripts.

354. **Memory Management** became an art form for PC gamers and power users, who would creatively edit CONFIG.SYS and AUTOEXEC.BAT to free up conventional memory to meet the minimum requirements of games like **"Descent" (1995)**, which required a significant amount of conventional memory to run.

355. **Batch File Menus**, created within AUTOEXEC.BAT, allowed users to select different startup configurations, useful for switching between gaming, productivity, or other setups that required different drivers and memory configurations.

356. **CD-ROM Drivers** in the early to mid-90s had to be loaded through CONFIG.SYS and AUTOEXEC.BAT, with lines like **LOADHIGH MSCDEX.EXE** becoming common sights in these files as CD-ROMs became prevalent for software and game distribution.

357. **Sound Card Settings**, such as setting the **BLASTER** environment variable in AUTOEXEC.BAT, were essential for DOS games to utilise sound properly. Users had to manually configure settings like IRQ, DMA, and I/O address for their sound cards.

358. The transition to **Windows 95** and beyond saw a decline in the necessity of manually editing these files, as the operating system handled much of the configuration

automatically. However, some advanced users and gamers continued to tweak AUTOEXEC.BAT and CONFIG.SYS for optimal performance and compatibility.

359. **CONFIG.SYS** could use the **DEVICEHIGH** and **LOADHIGH** commands to load drivers into high memory areas, freeing up more conventional memory for applications. This technique was essential for running memory-intensive programs within the 640KB conventional memory limit.

360. The advent of **boot menus** and **configuration managers** like **QEMM** and **MEMMAKER** helped automate the process of optimising memory, reducing the need for manual edits but still requiring a deep understanding of how DOS managed memory for those seeking to optimise their systems further.

361. Configuring Sound Blaster settings in the AUTOEXEC.BAT file was a common practice to ensure DOS games and applications could properly utilise the sound card's capabilities. Proper configuration was crucial for achieving sound in games, which added immensely to the gaming experience. Here's a detailed look at the settings:

    - **IRQ (Interrupt Request Line)**: This setting was used to specify the line over which the sound card would send interrupt signals to the CPU, signalling that it needed attention. Common IRQ settings for Sound Blaster cards were IRQ 5 or IRQ 7. The choice depended on avoiding conflicts with other devices, such as network cards or modems, which also required IRQ lines.

    - **DMA (Direct Memory Access)**: DMA channels were used to transfer data between the sound card and the system's memory without involving the CPU, allowing for smoother audio playback. Sound Blaster cards typically used DMA 1 for 8-bit sound and DMA 5 for 16-bit sound. Selecting a DMA channel that did not conflict

Making it Work: Machine Config

with other peripherals was crucial for preventing audio glitches or system instability.

- **I/O (Input/Output Address)**: The I/O address was used to define the memory location through which the CPU and the sound card communicated. Common I/O addresses for Sound Blaster cards included 0x220, 0x240, 0x260, and 0x280. The default and most commonly used I/O address was 0x220.

362. The **2 GB storage limit** was a significant barrier faced by users of the FAT16 file system, prevalent in early versions of Windows 95 and DOS. This limitation was due to FAT16's architecture, which could not support partitions larger than 2 GB, impacting users with growing storage needs.

363. To overcome the 2 GB limit, users and system administrators often partitioned larger hard drives into multiple smaller volumes, a workaround that allowed for the use of additional storage space but added complexity to file management and system organisation.

364. The introduction of **FAT32** with Windows 95 OSR2 (OEM Service Release 2) in 1996 provided a solution to the 2 GB limit, supporting larger partition sizes up to 2 terabytes (with a practical limit much lower due to cluster size), significantly increasing the storage capacity available to PCs without the need for multiple partitions.

365. The 2 GB limit also impacted users of database and multimedia applications, which required large amounts of contiguous storage space. Applications like video editing software and large databases were particularly affected, driving the need for file system improvements and larger storage solutions.

366. The transition beyond the 2 GB storage limit marked a critical point in the evolution of PC storage, coinciding with the increasing availability of larger hard drives and the growing demand for digital media storage, such as digital

photos, music, and video, which required more space than was previously common for personal computing.

367. The **8.3 filename convention** was a standard in DOS and early Windows operating systems, limiting filenames to a maximum of eight characters, followed by a dot, and three characters for the extension (e.g., example.txt). This convention stemmed from the limitations of the FAT file system used in these operating systems.

368. Creative abbreviations and acronyms became commonplace due to the 8.3 restriction, leading to cryptic filenames that required users to remember what each file contained. Software developers and users often had to come up with inventive ways to name files meaningfully within the eight-character limit.

369. The introduction of **Windows 95** and the FAT32 file system marked a significant departure from the 8.3 filename convention, supporting "long filenames" (LFN) up to 255 characters. This change allowed for more descriptive filenames, improving file management and usability.

370. Despite the move to long filenames, compatibility with older software and systems necessitated the creation of a "short name" alias for each file, adhering to the 8.3 format. This meant that even in newer versions of Windows, the 8.3 naming convention was still maintained behind the scenes for compatibility purposes.

371. The transition away from 8.3 filenames reflected the broader shift from command-line interfaces to graphical user interfaces (GUIs) in personal computing, where the limitations of the older system no longer aligned with the needs and capabilities of modern computer use and file management.

OPERATING SYSTEMS OF YORE

372. **MS-DOS**, or Microsoft Disk Operating System, was the foundation for PC computing in the 80s and early 90s, providing the platform upon which many of the era's most iconic software and games were run. It was known for its command-line interface, requiring users to type commands to execute tasks.

373. **DOS commands**, such as **DIR** for listing directory contents, **COPY** for copying files, and **DEL** for deleting files, became second nature to PC users. Mastery of these and other commands was essential for navigating and managing files in the DOS environment.

374. **Batch files (.bat)**, simple text files containing a series of DOS commands, were widely used for automating tasks, configuring system settings, and launching applications. They were a powerful tool for customising the computing experience.

375. **DOS-based networking** utilities, such as **Novell NetWare**, allowed for file and printer sharing among PCs in office environments, marking the early days of widespread computer networking in businesses.

376. The introduction of **Windows 95** marked the beginning of the end for DOS as the primary operating system for many users. While Windows 95 still relied on DOS for booting and certain operations, it introduced a graphical user interface (GUI) as the primary user interface, significantly changing how people interacted with their computers.

377. **MS-DOS Mode** in Windows 95 and 98 allowed users to reboot into a pure DOS environment for running older applications and games that were not compatible with Windows, highlighting the transition period where both DOS and Windows coexisted.

Operating Systems of Yore

378. The **DOS Prompt** or **Command Prompt** in later versions of Windows maintained the legacy of DOS, providing a command-line interface for advanced system management, troubleshooting, and automation tasks, long after DOS itself ceased to be the primary operating system for most users.

379. **4DOS** was an alternative command line interpreter for DOS, developed by JP Software, offering a wealth of features and enhancements over the standard DOS command prompt. It was designed to improve productivity and usability for power users with features like advanced batch file capabilities and command history.

380. One of the key features of 4DOS was its **enhanced batch programming capabilities**, including improved flow control, looping constructs, and the ability to create more complex and interactive scripts. This made it a favourite among DOS power users for automating tasks and customising their computing environment.

381. **4DOS introduced the concept of command aliases**, allowing users to define shortcuts for long or frequently used commands. This feature significantly sped up daily tasks and reduced typing, a precursor to modern command line customisation found in shells like Bash.

382. **Tab completion** was another significant usability improvement brought by 4DOS, enabling users to start typing a file or command name and then press Tab to automatically complete it. This feature, now taken for granted in modern operating systems, was a major time-saver and helped reduce typos and errors when navigating directories or running commands.

383. 4DOS also offered an **enhanced directory navigation system**, including the ability to display directories in a tree structure with the **TREE** command, providing users with a clearer view of their file system's organisation and making file management more intuitive.

384. Despite the decline of DOS as the primary operating system in the late 90s, **4DOS maintained a loyal user base** due to its powerful features and customisation options. It continued to be used in DOS-based environments and by enthusiasts running DOS applications within Windows or on dedicated legacy systems.

385. **OS/2**, developed by IBM and initially in collaboration with Microsoft, was introduced in 1987 as an operating system for PCs that was intended to eventually replace DOS and Windows.

386. **Windows 3.0 (1990)** introduced a graphical user interface (GUI) that was more user-friendly than its predecessors, featuring Program Manager and File Manager, marking a significant shift towards the GUI-dominated computing era.

387. The release of **OS/2 2.0** in 1992, dubbed a "better Windows than Windows" by some, introduced a fully pre-emptive multitasking environment and a 32-bit flat memory model, distinguishing it from the co-operative multitasking and 16-bit segments used by Windows at the time.

388. **OS/2's Workplace Shell**, introduced with version 2.0, was a graphical user interface that was object-oriented, offering a significant usability enhancement over the Program Manager interface in Windows 3.1.

389. **Despite its technical superiority in many areas**, such as stability and multitasking capabilities, OS/2 struggled to gain a significant market share against Windows, partly due to limited application support and IBM's marketing strategy.

390. **Windows 3.1 (1992)** added support for TrueType fonts, making it easier for users to work with a variety of typefaces, significantly enhancing document and presentation design on PCs.

391. **Windows 3.11 for Workgroups (1993)** added native network support, facilitating easier sharing of files and printers in office environments.

392. **Windows NT 3.1 (1993)** marked Microsoft's entry into the enterprise operating system market, designed to be more robust and secure than the consumer-oriented versions.

393. **OS/2 Warp 3**, released in 1994, attempted to address the lack of applications by including a "BonusPak" of useful software and offering better compatibility with Windows 3.1 applications, along with Internet support in an era when the Internet was becoming increasingly important.

394. **Windows 95 (1995)** was a landmark release that introduced the Start menu, taskbar, and minimise/maximise/close buttons on windows, elements of the user interface that are still recognisable today.

395. **OS/2 Warp 4**, introduced in 1996, included voice navigation and control features, an innovative addition at the time, allowing users to open applications, navigate the desktop, and dictate text through speech.

396. IBM marketed OS/2 Warp as a "better DOS than DOS and a better Windows than Windows", trying to capitalise on its ability to run DOS, Windows 3.1, and OS/2 applications, but this strategy often confused consumers about the OS's identity and value proposition.

397. **Windows NT 4.0 (1996)** combined the Windows 95 user interface with the robustness of the NT architecture, offering improved performance and security for business users.

398. **Windows 98 (1998)** introduced the Windows Driver Model (WDM) and support for USB devices, significantly improving hardware compatibility and ease of peripheral connection.

Operating Systems of Yore

399. **Windows 98 Lite** was an unofficial, stripped-down version of Windows 98, created by enthusiasts to remove unwanted components and improve system performance on less powerful hardware.

400. **Windows 98 SE (Second Edition, 1999)** added Internet Sharing, improved WDM support, and Internet Explorer 5, enhancing internet connectivity and browsing experiences.

401. One of OS/2's strengths was its robustness in handling network and server tasks, making it a preferred choice for ATM machines, banking systems, and other enterprise-level applications where stability and reliability were paramount.

402. **The OS/2 file system, HPFS (High Performance File System)**, offered several advantages over FAT used by DOS and Windows, such as support for long filenames and improved performance on large disks, though it also contributed to compatibility issues with other operating systems.

403. **Despite IBM's efforts, the withdrawal of Microsoft's support after version 1.3** and the rapid development of Windows 95 and NT created an insurmountable challenge for OS/2, leading to its decline as a mainstream operating system by the late '90s.

404. **IBM officially discontinued support for OS/2 in 2006**, but the OS has lived on in niche applications and among a small but dedicated community of enthusiasts who continue to use and develop for it under the ArcaOS continuation project.

405. **Windows Plus! 95 (1995)** and **Windows Plus! 98 (1998)** were add-on packs offering additional themes, games, and utilities, like DriveSpace, to enhance the user experience.

406. **Windows 95's launch** was accompanied by a massive marketing campaign, including a notable television

Operating Systems of Yore

commercial featuring the Rolling Stones' song "Start Me Up" to highlight the new Start button feature.

407. **Pre-emptive multitasking**, introduced to mainstream personal computing with Windows 95, marked a significant evolution from the cooperative multitasking of earlier Windows versions, allowing the operating system to better manage running applications and allocate system resources more efficiently.

408. The shift to pre-emptive multitasking enabled users to run multiple applications simultaneously with less risk of a single misbehaving app freezing the entire system, significantly improving the reliability and user experience of Windows.

409. **Internet Explorer 4.0**, integrated into Windows 98, introduced the Active Desktop feature, allowing web content to be displayed directly on the desktop, albeit with mixed reception from users due to security concerns.

410. **The Microsoft Office Suite**, tightly integrated with Windows 95 and later versions, became the de facto software package for word processing, spreadsheets, and presentations, cementing Microsoft's dominance in both operating systems and office software.

411. **User Account Control (UAC)**, introduced in later versions like Windows NT, began the process of providing finer control over user permissions, contributing to improved security by limiting software installation and system changes to authorised users.

412. **Solitaire (Windows 3.0, 1990)** was introduced to teach users how to drag and drop with a mouse, becoming an iconic time-waster and one of the most played PC games.

413. **Minesweeper (Windows 3.1, 1992)**, another classic, was designed to train users in precision mouse control and fast clicking, evolving into a beloved puzzle game with a dedicated fanbase.

414. **Hearts (Windows for Workgroups 3.1, 1992)** brought the popular card game to PCs, encouraging users to become familiar with the Windows network capabilities by allowing multiplayer games over a LAN.

415. **FreeCell (Windows 95, 1995)** was included not just for entertainment but also as a challenge; Microsoft reportedly received very few, if any, reports of unsolvable decks among the 32,000 included, showcasing the game's depth.

416. **3D Pinball for Windows – Space Cadet (Windows NT 4.0, 1995)** originally part of the Microsoft Plus! for Windows 95 pack, became a staple for its engaging gameplay and was a showcase for Windows' graphical capabilities.

417. **SkiFree (Windows Entertainment Pack, 1991)**, though not included with the OS, became widely played on Windows systems, famous for the yeti that chases the skier, becoming a piece of pop culture.

418. **Hover! (Windows 95, 1995)**, included on the Windows 95 installation CD-ROM, was a 3D game that showcased the operating system's capabilities for handling graphics and sound, offering capture-the-flag-style gameplay.

419. **Chip's Challenge (Windows Entertainment Pack, 1991)**, though initially not bundled with Windows, gained a significant following as part of the entertainment packs, challenging players with puzzles that required logical thinking and planning.

420. **Rodent's Revenge (Windows Entertainment Pack, 1991)**, another game from the entertainment packs, had players as a mouse trapping cats in puzzles, showcasing simple yet addicting gameplay mechanics.

421. **Internet Backgammon, Internet Checkers, and Internet Hearts (Windows 98, 1998)** were among the first games to utilise the Internet for multiplayer experiences directly from the Windows operating system, paving the way for future online gaming developments.

Operating Systems of Yore

422. **Microsoft Plus! for Windows 95 (1995)** introduced the concept of desktop themes to Windows users, allowing them to customise their desktops with coordinated sets of wallpapers, icons, cursors, and sounds. This add-on pack included several themes, such as "Dangerous Creatures," "Inside Your Computer," and "Leonardo da Vinci," that became instantly recognisable and fondly remembered.

423. **Desktop themes** became a way for users to personalise their computing experience significantly, with themes ranging from serene landscapes to science fiction and fantasy. Each theme offered a unique aesthetic, transforming the look and feel of the Windows interface and making the PC feel more personal and engaging.

424. **The "Mystery" theme**, included in Microsoft Plus! for Windows 98, featured a haunted house theme complete with eerie sounds and a mysterious wallpaper, showcasing the creative and sometimes whimsical possibilities of desktop customisation.

425. Third-party themes and utilities, such as **WindowBlinds** and **LiteStep**, emerged to provide even more customisation options beyond what was officially offered by Microsoft. These tools allowed for the modification of nearly every aspect of the Windows interface, catering to the desire for a more personalised and distinctive desktop environment.

426. **Active Desktop**, introduced with Internet Explorer 4.0 and Windows 98, allowed users to integrate web content directly onto their desktops. This feature could be used in conjunction with desktop themes to create dynamic backgrounds that could display live web pages, further expanding the customisation possibilities.

427. The popularity of customising desktop themes in the 90s laid the groundwork for future versions of Windows, which continued to offer and expand personalisation options, recognising the user's desire to tailor their computing environment to their tastes and interests.

428. **Disk Defragmenter (Defrag)** was a critical utility in the 90s, used to optimise the performance of hard drives by reorganising fragmented data so that files were stored in contiguous sectors. The visual representation of defrag in action, with its moving blocks and color-coded legend, became an iconic image of PC maintenance for many users.

429. **ScanDisk** was another essential utility, introduced with MS-DOS 6.2 and included in Windows 95 and later versions. It checked and repaired file systems and bad sectors on the hard disk, often running automatically after an improper shutdown to ensure the integrity of the file system.

430. Running **Defrag** was often a time-consuming process, requiring hours to complete on larger drives filled with data. It was common advice to run defrag overnight to avoid interrupting computer use during the day.

431. **ScanDisk's** surface scan feature was notorious for its length, especially on larger drives, but it was a critical step in diagnosing and fixing hard drive issues. Users frequently encountered the "ScanDisk is checking your hard drive for errors" message following an unexpected reboot.

432. The introduction of **NTFS (New Technology File System)** with Windows NT and its adoption in Windows XP reduced the necessity of frequent defragmentation due to its improved handling of file fragmentation, marking the beginning of the end for manual defrag routines.

433. **Windows Disk Cleanup** utility, introduced in Windows 98, helped users free up disk space by removing temporary files, emptying the Recycle Bin, and deleting other unnecessary files. This utility became a staple in the maintenance routine of PC users.

434. With the advent of **SSDs (Solid State Drives)** and advancements in operating system design, utilities like Defrag and ScanDisk became less critical for everyday

Operating Systems of Yore

users. Modern systems automatically manage these tasks in the background, with SSDs eliminating the need for defragmentation entirely due to their different data storage mechanism.

435. **SpinRite**, developed by Steve Gibson of Gibson Research Corporation (GRC), is a renowned disk recovery and maintenance tool that gained popularity in the 90s. It was designed to recover data from failing hard drives, rejuvenate aging drives, and maintain optimal performance by detecting and reassigning bad sectors before they resulted in data loss.

436. **CTRL+ALT+DELETE** was originally designed to reboot IBM PCs quickly without powering them off. David Bradley, one of the engineers who worked on the IBM PC, created this command. Its original purpose was to allow developers to restart their computers quickly during the development process.

437. In the Windows operating system, starting with **Windows 3.0** and becoming more prominent in **Windows 95**, CTRL+ALT+DELETE evolved into a command to bring up the Task Manager or the Windows Security screen, allowing users to close unresponsive programs or log out.

438. The key combination became known as the "three-finger salute" among computer users due to its frequent use to recover from system freezes or to safely terminate applications that were not responding.

439. **Bill Gates** has been quoted as saying that making CTRL+ALT+DELETE a necessary step for logging into a Windows PC (a feature introduced with Windows NT 3.1) was a mistake, albeit one that enhanced security by requiring a physical interaction to initiate the login process, reducing the risk of automated password entry through software.

440. Over the years, CTRL+ALT+DELETE has become an iconic part of PC culture, symbolising a quick fix for

computer issues and even entering the broader lexicon as a metaphor for starting over or resetting a situation.

441. The **Windows Registry** was introduced with Windows 3.1 as a system to centralise configurations and settings for both the operating system and applications, replacing the need for multiple INI files scattered across the system.

442. Advanced users and IT professionals in the 90s often tweaked the Windows Registry to optimise system performance or enable hidden features.

443. The complexity and sensitivity of the Windows Registry led to the creation of a common mantra among tech enthusiasts: **"Backup your registry before making changes"**, highlighting the potential for system instability or failure if errors were made.

444. **Registry Editor (RegEdit)** became an essential utility for directly editing the registry, providing a graphical interface for navigating and modifying registry keys and values.

445. Windows 95's introduction of **Plug and Play (PnP)** was a significant step forward in driver management, promising easier installation and configuration of hardware.

446. **OS/2**, despite its robust multitasking and stability, struggled with hardware driver support as many manufacturers prioritised Windows, leaving users and IBM to fill in the gaps. This situation highlighted the challenge of competing in an ecosystem dominated by Microsoft.

447. **Apple's Mac OS** in the '90s maintained a more controlled hardware ecosystem, which allowed for better driver integration and stability but limited the range of supported peripherals compared to the PC world, reflecting Apple's approach to balancing control and user experience.

448. The rise of 3D graphics accelerators in the late '90s led to a driver arms race among manufacturers like NVIDIA, ATI, and 3dfx, with frequent updates to optimise performance

and compatibility with an expanding library of games and applications, marking the early days of the GPU driver updates that gamers today are very familiar with.

449. The advent of the Internet towards the late '90s transformed the cumbersome process of obtaining the latest hardware drivers, moving from distributing updates via floppy disks or CD-ROMs mailed by manufacturers, to downloading them directly from company websites.

FLOPPY TO CD: SOFTWARE EVOLUTION

450. The word **"Loading"**, often accompanied by a progress bar or animated graphic, was a common sight in 90s PC software, signalling that the application was being loaded into memory from slower storage mediums like floppy disks or CD-ROMs. This could take from a few seconds to several minutes, depending on the software's size and the computer's processing speed.

451. **Loading screens** in PC games of the era were not just practical indicators that game assets were being prepared but also opportunities for developers to present artwork, tips, lore, or creative animations. This added an element of engagement and anticipation for the user during the wait time.

452. The phrase **"Now Loading"** became synonymous with the experience of using larger, more complex software or games that required significant time to load due to the limitations of hardware and storage technology at the time. Applications like **Adobe Photoshop** and large-scale games such as **"Myst"** exemplified this, where loading times were a momentary pause in the creative process or gameplay.

453. During the early days of the internet, the term **"Loading"** was also commonplace on web pages, especially those rich in images or multimedia content. Users on dial-up connections often faced lengthy waits, contrasting sharply with today's near-instantaneous web access.

454. **Keyboard overlays** were thin plastic sheets or cardboard cut outs that sat over a computer keyboard, providing quick reference for software-specific commands. They were especially popular with complex software applications and

games that utilised numerous keyboard shortcuts for operations, enhancing usability and learning for users.

455. **Flight simulators** like **"Microsoft Flight Simulator"** in the 90s often came with keyboard overlays, helping pilots quickly find the myriad of controls needed to simulate flying an aircraft accurately. These overlays were invaluable for enhancing the realism and immersion of the simulation experience without memorising extensive command lists.

456. **Music production software** and **Digital Audio Workstations (DAWs)** also utilised keyboard overlays to give users quick access to shortcuts for editing, mixing, and navigation. Programs like **"Cakewalk"** and **"Pro Tools"** had overlays that mapped out complex functions, streamlining the creative process for composers and producers.

457. Overlays not only served a practical purpose but also acted as a form of physical customisation for the user's workspace, making each setup unique to the software most frequently used. This personal touch added to the sense of ownership and expertise over one's computing environment.

458. With the advent of more intuitive user interfaces and the increase in on-screen help and tutorials, the need for physical keyboard overlays has diminished. However, they remain a nostalgic reminder of a time when software required more from its users in terms of memorisation and command execution.

459. **WordStar** was one of the earliest word processing programs to gain popularity on personal computers, originally released in the late 1970s. By the 90s, it was known for its complex command sequences that, while powerful, had a steep learning curve compared to more visually intuitive interfaces of later word processors.

460. Despite its declining user base in the 90s due to the rise of more GUI-oriented programs like Microsoft Word,

WordStar retained a loyal following among writers and professionals who valued its keyboard-centric approach to document creation, allowing for fast, efficient editing without reaching for the mouse.

461. WordStar's **non-document mode**, a feature that allowed users to navigate and edit text without affecting the document's formatting, was particularly appreciated by writers and editors who needed to focus on content over appearance during the initial stages of writing.

462. The program's influence extended beyond its own lifespan; **George R.R. Martin**, author of the "A Song of Ice and Fire" series, famously continued to use WordStar on a DOS machine for his writing, citing its simplicity and lack of distractions as key to his productivity.

463. WordStar's command set, including the renowned "diamond" of cursor movement keys (Ctrl-S for left, Ctrl-D for right, Ctrl-E for up, and Ctrl-X for down), became so ingrained in the muscle memory of its users that some sought out emulation software or custom keyboard mappings to replicate the experience in modern word processing applications.

464. **Lotus 1-2-3** was a dominant spreadsheet program for MS-DOS in the early 1990s, often credited with making the IBM PC a staple in corporate offices for its powerful data management and analysis features.

465. The software was part of the Lotus SmartSuite, which included other productivity tools like Lotus Word Pro and Lotus Organizer, aiming to compete with Microsoft Office.

466. A notable characteristic of Lotus 1-2-3 was its keystroke-driven commands, which differed from the mouse-driven interface popularised later by Windows applications. This made it highly efficient for experienced users.

467. Lotus 1-2-3's integration capabilities, allowing users to pull in data from databases and other applications, set a

Floppy to CD: Software Evolution

precedent for software interoperability in the business world.

468. The transition from Lotus 1-2-3 to Excel as the leading spreadsheet software marked a significant shift in the late 1990s, largely due to Microsoft's aggressive strategy of bundling Office with Windows, showcasing the intense competition in the software market.

469. The release of Windows 3.1 in 1992 introduced **TrueType fonts** to the masses, enabling WYSIWYG (What You See Is What You Get) printing and screen display. This was a major advancement in desktop publishing on personal computers.

470. **Comic Sans MS**, created by Vincent Connare in 1994, quickly became one of the most iconic (and controversial) fonts of the 90s. It was designed for Microsoft Bob but ended up being included in Windows 95, intended for informal documents and children's materials.

471. The 90s saw the rise of digital font foundries like FontShop (founded in 1989) and Emigre, which were pivotal in introducing distinctive and experimental fonts that defined the visual culture of the era, such as Matrix and Template Gothic.

472. **Arial**, often criticised for its similarities to Helvetica, became ubiquitous in the 90s after being included in Windows 3.1 as a core font. It was used widely in both professional and casual digital documents, symbolising the era's shift towards digital typesetting.

473. The use of fonts like **Times New Roman** and **Courier New** as default text in word processing software like Microsoft Word shaped the look of countless documents in the 90s, from school papers to corporate reports, marking the beginning of standardised digital document formats.

474. **Anti-aliasing** became a significant feature in graphic design and desktop publishing software in the 1990s, as it greatly improved the appearance of text and graphics by smoothing out the jagged edges that are typical of pixelated images.

475. The introduction of **"Adobe Photoshop 3.0"** in 1994, with its advanced anti-aliasing capabilities for text, marked a turning point for professional graphic designers, allowing for the creation of smoother and more visually appealing digital text and imagery.

476. In the realm of video games, anti-aliasing techniques started to be implemented in the late 90s to enhance the visual quality of 3D graphics on personal computers, reducing the "jaggies" that were prominent in early 3D games. Games like **"Quake II" (1997)** and **"Unreal" (1998)** were among the first to offer such features, pushing the boundaries of PC gaming graphics.

477. The adoption of anti-aliasing in operating systems' user interfaces began with **Mac OS 8** in 1997, which introduced font smoothing. This was a precursor to more sophisticated text rendering techniques in later operating systems, influencing the aesthetic standards of GUIs in the following decades.

478. **Windows File Manager** was first introduced in Windows 3.0 in 1990, serving as a revolutionary way for users to navigate and manage their files in a graphical interface, moving away from the command-line interfaces of MS-DOS.

479. File Manager allowed users to perform file operations like moving, copying, and deleting within a two-pane interface, which was a significant usability improvement over the previous MS-DOS command line commands.

480. The integration of network functionality into File Manager in later versions of Windows for Workgroups enabled users to easily access and manage files across a local area

network (LAN), highlighting the beginning of widespread networked computing in offices.

481. In the mid-90s, with the release of Windows 95, File Manager was replaced by **Windows Explorer**, which introduced the "tree-view" directory structure and integrated web browsing capabilities, marking the end of the standalone File Manager era.

482. Despite its replacement, File Manager remained a fond memory for many early PC users for its simplicity and efficiency, symbolising the transition from text-based to graphical user interfaces in personal computing.

483. **Microsoft Encarta** was introduced in 1993 as one of the first digital multimedia encyclopaedias available on CD-ROM, offering a wealth of knowledge through text, images, videos, and interactive maps, revolutionising access to information beyond traditional books.

484. Encarta was known for its "MindMaze" game, a trivia game set in a medieval castle, which became a beloved feature for many users, blending education with entertainment and making learning fun for children and adults alike.

485. The **Encarta World Atlas**, included in later versions, was a highly praised feature that provided detailed geographic information, interactive maps, and tools for exploring the world, reflecting the growing interest in global awareness and education through technology.

486. **PaintShop Pro**, developed by Jasc Software, emerged in the early 90s as a powerful and affordable alternative to more expensive image editing software, gaining popularity among amateur and professional digital artists for its comprehensive set of tools.

487. The software was initially released as shareware in 1990, allowing users to try before they buy, a distribution model that contributed significantly to its widespread adoption and community support.

488. PaintShop Pro was known for its low system requirements, making advanced photo editing accessible to users with less powerful PCs, a crucial factor in its popularity during the early days of digital photography and home computing.

489. One of the standout features of PaintShop Pro was its plugin support, which allowed users to extend its functionality with third-party filters and effects, fostering a vibrant ecosystem of enhancements that catered to a wide range of creative needs.

490. The release of PaintShop Pro 5 in 1998 introduced layers, a feature now considered fundamental in digital image editing, which significantly expanded the software's capabilities for complex compositions and detailed graphic work.

491. **CorelDRAW**, first released in 1989, quickly became a favourite among graphic designers for its vector graphics editing capabilities, marking a significant shift towards digital design in the pre-Adobe Illustrator dominance era.

492. The software was notable for its comprehensive suite, which included **Corel PHOTO-PAINT** for bitmap editing and **CorelSHOW** for creating slide shows, offering an all-in-one solution for graphic design and desktop publishing needs.

493. CorelDRAW's inclusion of clipart and fonts was a significant selling point, providing users with a wealth of resources right out of the box, which was especially valuable in an era before widespread internet access made such resources easily available online.

494. **Clipart** became a staple of personal and professional digital documents in the 90s, with **Microsoft Office** and **CorelDRAW** offering extensive libraries of clipart to enhance the visual appeal of everything from presentations to party invitations.

495. The proliferation of CD-ROMs in the 90s meant that clipart collections could be vast and varied, with discs often packed with thousands of images, enabling users to find clipart for almost any occasion or subject matter.

496. **Pegasus Mail**, one of the earliest email clients, was widely used in academic and corporate environments in the 90s due to its robust handling of multiple accounts and strong support for networked installations, particularly on **Novell NetWare** networks.

497. **Eudora**, launched in 1988, became a popular email client for both Windows and Macintosh users by offering a user-friendly interface and advanced features like filtering and support for multiple mailboxes, making it a favourite in the burgeoning days of personal internet use.

498. **Microsoft Outlook**, introduced as part of the **Microsoft Office** suite in 1997, quickly became a dominant email client in corporate settings, integrating email with calendar and contact management features, and setting the standard for office communication tools.

499. **Netscape Communicator**'s mail client, part of the **Netscape Navigator** suite in the mid-90s, was notable for integrating web browsing and email into a single application, reflecting the internet's growing importance in everyday computing and communication.

500. **Internet Explorer (IE)** was launched by Microsoft in 1995 and quickly became one of the most used web browsers, due in part to its inclusion with the Windows operating system, which contributed to its dominance in the browser wars of the late 90s.

501. **Netscape Navigator**, introduced in 1994, was the leading web browser before the rise of IE. Its user-friendly interface and pioneering technologies like cookies and JavaScript made it the browser of choice for early internet users.

502. The release of **Internet Explorer 4** in 1997 was marked by a highly publicised launch event, including a giant "E" logo placed in the yard of Netscape's headquarters, symbolising the intense competition between Microsoft and Netscape.

503. **Opera**, launched in 1996, distinguished itself with features like speed dial and tabbed browsing, which were innovative at the time and influenced the development of web browsers that followed.

504. Microsoft's integration of Internet Explorer with the Windows operating system led to a landmark antitrust lawsuit in 1998, with the U.S. Department of Justice accusing Microsoft of using its operating system monopoly to stifle competition in the browser market, significantly impacting the company's business practices and the broader tech industry.

505. **Macromedia Flash**, originally released in 1996, revolutionised web content by enabling the creation and delivery of rich animations, interactive media, and full-fledged web applications, making it a cornerstone of dynamic content in the late 90s.

506. **Norton Utilities**, a suite of disk and system utilities designed to optimise and maintain system performance, was a must-have for Windows users looking to protect their data and enhance their PC's efficiency.

507. **Adaptec Easy CD Creator**, essential for the burgeoning CD-RW drives in home PCs, allowed users to create music CDs, back up data, and make duplicates.

508. **ZoneAlarm**, a personal firewall application introduced in the late 90s, became crucial for many internet users to protect their PCs from hackers and network intrusions.

509. **Daemon Tools**, released in the late 90s, allowed users to mount disc images as virtual CD/DVD drives, facilitating the use of CD-based software without the physical disc.

510. **Tweak UI**, part of Microsoft's **PowerToys for Windows 95**, enabled users to customise hidden settings of the Windows interface, from menu speed to login procedures, showcasing the desire for deeper personalisation and control over the computing environment.

511. **UltraEdit**, first released in 1994, became the text editor of choice for many programmers and web developers, offering robust editing features for a wide range of file types and programming languages, emphasising the era's diversification of software development tools.

512. **Rainmeter**, while gaining prominence in the 2000s, began development in the late 90s as a tool for customising the desktop environment with skins that display real-time system performance data and other useful information, highlighting the personalisation trend in PC use.

513. **WinRAR**, introduced in 1995, became another essential tool for file compression, supporting a wide range of formats including its proprietary RAR format, known for its efficiency and compression ratio, catering to the needs for data storage and transfer optimisation.

514. **ACDSee**, launched in the mid-90s, was pivotal for digital photography enthusiasts, offering a fast, versatile way to view, organise, and edit images, signalling the digital transformation in photography and visual media management.

515. **After Dark** was a popular screensaver program for Macintosh and Windows systems, first released in 1989, best known for its iconic "Flying Toasters" screensaver, which featured toasters with wings flying across the screen, emblematic of the whimsical and creative software of the era.

516. The program offered a variety of animated screensavers, including "Bad Dog," "Fish World," and "Starry Night," allowing users to personalise their computers in a novel

and entertaining way, contributing to the cultural fabric of computer use in the 90s.

517. After Dark also introduced a feature called "Screen Antics," which included interactive screensavers like "You Bet Your Head" and games that could be played directly on the screensaver, blending utility with entertainment in a way that was innovative for its time.

518. **"Microsoft minutes"** became a tongue-in-cheek term among users to describe the unpredictable and frequently inaccurate time estimates provided by Windows for operations like copying files or installing software, where a task might initially be estimated to take several minutes but would finish either much more quickly or take significantly longer.

519. This phenomenon was particularly noticeable during the installation of Windows 95 and subsequent operating system updates, where the setup process could display a progress bar and time estimate that seemed to have little correlation with actual time passing.

520. **IRC (Internet Relay Chat)**, developed in 1988, became a foundational form of online communication in the 90s, allowing real-time text messaging in chat rooms organised by topic, which fostered a sense of global community and live interaction unprecedented at the time.

521. IRC was a precursor to modern social media and messaging platforms, with its network of servers and channels laying the groundwork for the concept of virtual spaces where users could gather based on shared interests.

522. IRC also saw the emergence of early internet bots, which could perform tasks ranging from moderating chat rooms to providing users with games or information services, demonstrating early examples of automated interaction within online communities.

523. **ICQ**, launched in 1996, was one of the first instant messaging (IM) clients to gain widespread popularity, introducing the concept of a "UIN" (Universal Internet Number) as a way for users to find and connect with each other, a departure from the use of email addresses or screen names.

524. **AIM (AOL Instant Messenger)**, introduced in 1997, popularised the use of "Buddy Lists" and away messages, features that would become staples in IM clients, reflecting the growing desire for more personalised and expressive forms of online communication.

525. **MSN Messenger**, launched by Microsoft in 1999, integrated with the Windows operating system and offered features like custom emoticons and nudge, pushing the boundaries of IM software capabilities and user interaction at the time.

526. **Mavis Beacon Teaches Typing**, first released in 1987, became the go-to software for learning typing skills, known for its adaptive lessons that adjusted to the user's skill level, making it a staple in both educational settings and homes.

527. Despite being a fictional character, Mavis Beacon became a recognisable face of typing education, with the software's box art and promotional materials featuring various models over the years to personify her, creating a unique brand identity in educational software.

528. The program included a variety of typing games, such as racing cars and navigating through mazes, which made learning to type fun and engaging, especially for younger users, setting a precedent for educational software that combines learning with gameplay.

529. **Dragon Dictate**, later known as **Dragon NaturallySpeaking**, was a pioneer in voice recognition technology, released in the early 90s. It allowed users to dictate text and control their computers with voice

commands, introducing a new way of interacting with personal computers.

530. The software required users to go through a voice training session, helping it to better recognise their speech patterns and accents, a process that, while time-consuming, was revolutionary in improving the accuracy of voice recognition.

531. Early versions of Dragon software were expensive and required a significant amount of system resources, reflecting the cutting-edge nature of speech recognition technology at the time and its initial positioning as a tool for professionals and users with specific accessibility needs.

532. Similar technologies, like IBM's **ViaVoice** and Microsoft's speech recognition integrated into Windows, followed suit, contributing to the development of voice-activated computing and laying the groundwork for today's voice assistants like Siri, Alexa, and Google Assistant.

533. **Nero Burning ROM**, launched in 1997, quickly became the go-to software for CD burning, allowing users to create music CDs, data backups, and eventually DVDs, embodying the era's shift towards digital media storage and sharing.

534. **RealPlayer**, launched by RealNetworks in 1995, was one of the first media players to support streaming audio and video over the internet, marking a significant leap forward in how multimedia content was consumed online.

535. Known for its ability to play RealAudio and RealVideo formats, RealPlayer became synonymous with early internet radio and video streaming, offering users a glimpse into the future of digital media consumption despite the limitations of dial-up connections.

536. **Winamp**, released in 1997 by Nullsoft, quickly became one of the most popular media players for Windows, celebrated for its customisable skins, vast plugin library, and playlist

feature, embodying the playful and experimental spirit of digital culture in the late 90s.

IN PRINT: COMPUTER MAGAZINES

537. **PC Magazine**, first published in 1982, was a seminal publication for PC enthusiasts, offering in-depth reviews, previews of upcoming technology, and tips and tricks for optimising computer use, becoming a trusted source for tech news and advice in the 90s.

538. **Byte** magazine, known for its technical depth, catered to a more technically savvy audience, offering insights into computer science, programming, and hardware developments, contributing significantly to the knowledge base of computing professionals and hobbyists alike.

539. The iconic "Demo Disk" or "Cover CD" included with many PC magazines, such as **PC World** and **Computer Gaming World**, provided readers with software trials, freeware, and game demos, becoming a highly anticipated feature that introduced users to new software and games each month.

540. Computer Gaming World magazine offered extensive coverage of PC games, including reviews, strategy guides, and developer interviews, playing a crucial role in the growth of PC gaming culture throughout the 90s.

541. **Wired** magazine, launched in 1993, brought a broader cultural perspective to technology reporting, blending discussions of the internet, digital culture, and technology's impact on society, and quickly became a symbol of the dot-com era's optimism.

542. The "Shareware" section in magazines like **PC Format** introduced many to affordable software options, allowing readers to sample and support independent software developers directly, fostering a community of innovation and collaboration.

In Print: Computer Magazines

543. Many PC magazines ran annual awards or "Editors' Choice" features, which were highly anticipated and influential in guiding consumer purchases, helping to establish the reputations of hardware and software products.

544. The rise of internet forums and online news in the late 90s and early 2000s began to diminish the influence and circulation of printed PC magazines, signalling a shift towards digital consumption of technology news and information.

545. Publications like **Linux Journal** and .**NET** magazine catered to niche audiences interested in open-source software and web development, respectively, highlighting the diversity of interests within the PC community.

546. The detailed tutorials and "how-to" articles found in magazines like **PC Mechanic** and **Maximum PC** demystified computer maintenance and upgrades for the layperson, empowering readers to build, customise, and repair their own systems.

547. **Mail ordering** via PC magazines was a primary method for acquiring software, hardware, and accessories in the 90s, with readers eagerly flipping through pages of ads and listings to find deals and new products, highlighting a time before e-commerce became dominant.

548. Advertisements and classified sections in magazines like **PC World** and **Computer Shopper** were densely packed with listings from various vendors, offering everything from the latest graphics cards to custom-built PCs, serving as a marketplace for tech enthusiasts to explore and purchase the latest tech.

549. Many PC enthusiasts relied on these ads to find niche or hard-to-find items, such as specific cables, components for custom builds, or software not carried in local stores, showcasing the importance of mail order catalogues in the pre-internet shopping era.

In Print: Computer Magazines

550. PC magazines in the 90s were treasure troves of tips and tricks for optimising Windows performance, with advice ranging from tweaking system settings to free up memory, to disabling unnecessary startup programs to speed up boot times, reflecting the hands-on approach users had to take to maintain their systems.

551. The "Easter eggs" sections in magazines like **PC Magazine** and **Macworld** highlighted hidden features or jokes within software and operating systems, such as the "Teapot" in Microsoft's DirectX diagnostics tool, fostering a culture of exploration and curiosity among users.

552. Cheat codes and strategy guides for PC games were regular features in gaming magazines like **Computer Gaming World** and **PC Gamer**, providing invaluable insights for navigating the challenging levels or unlocking secret content in games, contributing to the communal gaming culture of sharing knowledge and experiences.

553. Many magazines offered detailed how-to articles on installing new hardware, such as adding more RAM or upgrading a video card, complete with step-by-step instructions and photos, demystifying the process for those new to PC DIY projects.

554. Tips on using office software more efficiently, like shortcut keys for Microsoft Office or macros for automating tasks in Excel, were also common, aiming to improve productivity and enhance the user's software proficiency.

555. The troubleshooting Q&A sections, where readers could submit their tech problems to be answered by experts, were a crucial resource for solving common and obscure computer issues, showcasing the communal effort to navigate the complexities of PC technology.

TV SHOWS FOR THE TECHIE

556. **GamesMaster** was a pioneering British television show that aired from 1992 to 1998, blending video game reviews, news, and live challenges, becoming a cultural icon of the 90s gaming scene and one of the first shows to bring video gaming to mainstream television.

557. The show featured the "GamesMaster," a character played by **Sir Patrick Moore**, who provided gaming tips, cheats, and judged competitions, adding a unique blend of authority and theatricality to video game advice and entertainment.

558. Despite its end in the late 90s, GamesMaster left a lasting legacy, fondly remembered by a generation of gamers for its contribution to the gaming culture and community in the UK and beyond.

559. **The Computer Chronicles** was a pioneering American television series that aired from 1983 to 2002, offering viewers an in-depth look at the burgeoning world of computers, technology, and the internet, serving as a vital source of information during the personal computing boom of the 1980s and 90s.

560. Hosted by **Stewart Cheifet**, the show featured interviews, product reviews, and demos, covering a wide range of topics from the latest software developments to emerging internet technologies, making technology accessible to a broad audience.

561. **Bits** was a British television show that aired on Channel 4 from 1999 to 2001, focusing on video games and the gaming culture, offering a fresh and edgy perspective compared to more traditional gaming shows of the time, specifically targeting a young adult audience.

562. The show was notable for its all-female presenting team, including **Aleks Krotoski**, **Emily Newton Dunn**, and **Claudia Trimde**, a rarity in gaming media at the time, which helped to challenge the male-dominated perceptions of the gaming community.

563. **Video & Arcade Top 10** (often abbreviated to V&A Top 10) was a Canadian television show that aired from 1991 to 2006, becoming a staple for a generation of gamers by featuring live gameplay, video game reviews, tips, and cheat codes, primarily focusing on console games but reflecting the broader video game culture that also influenced PC gaming.

564. The show's hosts, including **Nicholas Picholas**, became familiar faces to Canadian youth, contributing to the program's friendly and engaging atmosphere, which encouraged a sense of community among viewers.

565. Despite its focus on console gaming, the cultural impact and popularity of "Video & Arcade Top 10" mirrored the growing interest in video games across all platforms, including PCs, during the 90s, contributing to the era's burgeoning video game fandom.

566. **Cybernet** was a weekly video game and technology television program that originated in the UK in the mid-90s, offering viewers a mix of video game reviews, previews, tips, cheats, and industry news, catering to a growing audience of gamers and tech enthusiasts.

567. Known for its concise format and robotic voiceover, "Cybernet" became popular not just in the UK but around the world, syndicated in various countries, which helped globalise gaming culture and information sharing before the widespread use of the internet.

568. **Nick Arcade**, a game show that aired on Nickelodeon from 1992 to 1993, innovatively combined video game challenges with physical competitions, making it a unique

TV Shows for the Techie

and memorable part of 90s children's programming, particularly for young gamers.

569. Contestants on "Nick Arcade" competed in arcade-style video games, trivia questions about video games, and a final round inside a virtual reality video game world, which was one of the earliest representations of virtual reality concepts on television.

570. **Beyond 2000** was an Australian television series that aired from 1985 to 1999, renowned for exploring future-focused technologies, innovations, and scientific breakthroughs, offering audiences around the world a glimpse into potential technological advancements and their impact on society.

571. The show covered a broad range of topics, from renewable energy sources and medical breakthroughs to the latest developments in computing and telecommunications, making it a source of education and inspiration for viewers fascinated by the possibilities of future technology.

572. **Bad Influence!** was a British television show that aired from 1992 to 1996, focusing on video games and computer technology, providing reviews, previews, and the latest news in gaming and computer innovations, appealing to young tech enthusiasts of the era.

573. The show's presenters, including **Violet Berlin**, became iconic figures in the UK gaming community, respected for their knowledge and enthusiasm for technology, making "Bad Influence!" a trusted source of information and entertainment for a generation of gamers and tech enthusiasts.

574. Violet Berlin also made cameo appearances in several video games, most notably in **Micro Machines 2: Turbo Tournament (1994)** as a playable character, cementing her status as a gaming icon and bridging the gap between television presenting and the gaming world she covered.

TV Shows for the Techie

575. **Electric Playground**, also known as "EP," was a Canadian television series that premiered in 1997, dedicated to covering the video game industry, including PC games, with reviews, previews, interviews, and behind-the-scenes looks at game development, becoming a valued source for gamers seeking the latest in gaming news.

576. The show was co-created and hosted by **Victor Lucas**, who became a well-respected figure in the gaming community for his in-depth knowledge and passion for video games, contributing to the show's reputation for providing comprehensive and enthusiastic coverage of the gaming world.

577. **GamePro TV** was a television show that aired in the early 1990s, based on the popular **GamePro** magazine, bringing video game news, reviews, and tips from the pages to the screen, serving as an early multimedia extension of video game journalism.

578. Hosted by **J.D. Roth**, GamePro TV provided an energetic and entertaining format for delivering the latest in video game culture to a young audience, including segments on cheat codes, game strategies, and previews of upcoming games, reflecting the growing influence of video games in youth culture.

579. The show's tie-in with GamePro magazine allowed for a cross-platform approach to gaming content, with viewers able to read more about what they saw on TV in the magazine, fostering a community around the GamePro brand during the early days of gaming fandom.

580. Despite its relatively short run, GamePro TV left a lasting impression on its viewers by being one of the first shows to treat video games as a significant and newsworthy form of entertainment, paving the way for future gaming shows and the evolution of video game media.

REEL TECH: MOVIES WITH 90S COMPUTING

581. **"Sneakers"** released in 1992, is a heist film that delves into the world of espionage, hacking, and cryptography, featuring a team of security specialists tasked with retrieving a powerful decryption device, highlighting the growing public fascination with computer security and the potential for technology to both protect and invade privacy.

582. The movie showcased the concept of "social engineering" as a hacking technique, demonstrating how trickery and manipulation of people can be as effective as technical hacking skills, a method that remains highly relevant in today's cybersecurity landscape.

583. "Sneakers" emphasised the importance of encryption and the potential consequences of powerful decryption tools falling into the wrong hands, foretelling modern debates over encryption, privacy, and national security.

584. A memorable moment in **"Jurassic Park"**, released in 1993, is when the young character Lex uses a computer to navigate the park's security system, famously declaring, "It's a UNIX system! I know this!" – but was it though?

585. **"The Net"**, released in 1995, starred Sandra Bullock as a software engineer who stumbles upon a conspiracy that erases her identity, showcasing early Hollywood interpretations of the internet and cybersecurity, which were burgeoning concepts to the general public at the time.

586. The film depicted technologies such as online chat rooms, hacking, and the potential dangers of digital identity theft, prophetic themes that have become increasingly relevant in today's digital age, reflecting growing concerns about privacy and security online.

587. "The Net" used floppy disks containing a "gateway" program as a plot device, illustrating the era's reliance on physical media for software distribution and data storage, a concept that seems quaint in the age of cloud computing and online data storage.

588. The portrayal of the internet as a vast, unregulated network where identity can be easily manipulated or erased resonated with 90s audiences beginning to grapple with the implications of living life online, highlighting the film's role in shaping perceptions of digital culture and the potential dark sides of technology.

589. **"Hackers"**, released in 1995, became iconic for its stylised portrayal of the cyberpunk subculture and hacking community, presenting a fantastical vision of young hackers battling corporate corruption, which captivated audiences with its vivid depiction of cyberspace and hacker ethics.

590. Despite its exaggerated portrayal of hacking techniques and computer technology, "Hackers" introduced many to the concept of cybersecurity threats, such as viruses and worms, at a time when the internet was becoming integral to daily life, raising awareness about the potential dangers lurking in the digital world.

591. "Hackers" featured a memorable scene where characters use a payphone and a laptop to make a free long-distance call by emulating the sound of coins dropping, a nod to the practice of "phreaking," showcasing the ingenuity attributed to hackers in exploiting telecommunications systems.

ECHOES OF A DECADE: THE QUINTESSENTIAL SOUNDS OF 90S PCS

592. The iconic sound of a **dial-up modem connecting to the internet**, often described as a sequence of beeps, hisses, and static, became a defining auditory hallmark of the 90s internet experience, symbolising the anticipation and sometimes frustration of waiting to get online.

    This sequence of sounds during a dial-up modem's handshake was not just noise but a crucial part of the negotiation process between the modem and the internet service provider's (ISP) system, with each sound representing a step in the protocol for establishing a stable connection.

593. The phrase **"your sound card is working perfectly"** is famously associated with the Windows Sound System configuration test in Windows 3.1 and later versions, serving as a reassuring audio confirmation that the computer's sound capabilities were set up correctly.

594. The phrase **"You've got mail"** became synonymous with AOL (America Online), greeting users receiving new emails, and has since been humorously mimicked in various forms of media, reflecting its deep cultural imprint as one of the internet's earliest and most recognisable sounds.

    It was so emblematic of the online experience in the 90s that it inspired the title of the 1998 romantic comedy "You've Got Mail," starring Tom Hanks and Meg Ryan, further cementing its place in pop culture.

595. The **"tada"** sound from Windows is famously known as the system startup sound in Windows 3.1, greeting users with a triumphant musical flourish as they booted up their

computers with a sense of accomplishment in an era when computer crashes and issues were more common.

This startup chime, along with other system sounds from the era, was composed by Microsoft sound designer Brian Eno for Windows 95, marking a significant shift towards creating a more user-friendly and emotionally resonant computing experience, with Eno crafting the sound to be "optimistic and futuristic."

596. The distinctive grinding and whirring noises of **floppy drives** while reading and writing data were often humorously anthropomorphised by users, with some joking that the drives were "chewing" on the floppy disks.

    The **Floppotron** on Paweł Zadrożniak's YouTube channel has gained a significant following, where its renditions of popular songs, movie themes, and video game music have captivated audiences worldwide, demonstrating the enduring appeal and cultural legacy of vintage computing.

597. The iconic **"Uh Oh!"** sound notification of ICQ became synonymous with receiving a message, embedding itself in the collective memory of its user base and becoming a defining sound of online communication in the late 90s.

598. The Winamp startup sound, which famously declared, **"Winamp, it really whips the llama's ass!"** became a humorous and memorable catchphrase that epitomised the quirky, irreverent spirit of 90s software culture, often surprising first-time users with its unexpectedness and contributing to the player's cult status.

599. The distinct sound of **dot matrix printers**, characterised by a rhythmic buzzing and whirring as the print head moved back and forth, was a common backdrop in offices and some homes, instantly recognisable and often associated with productivity or late-night homework sessions.

Echoes of a Decade: The Quintessential Sounds of 90s PCs

600. The unexpected "beep" of **incoming SMS messages** on PC speakers, caused by interference picked up by the speakers from cellular signals, became an unintended yet familiar sound for many, signalling an incoming message or call on a nearby mobile phone.

601. **The sharp "pop" heard when turning on speakers** connected to a PC or stereo system was a common experience, marking the beginning of a computing session, a gaming adventure, or a music listening session.

602. The celebratory **cascade of cards** at the end of a winning game of Solitaire on Windows became a symbol of procrastination and small victories in the workplace, often regarded as the most productivity many users achieved during the workday, highlighting the game's role as a beloved time-waster and stress reliever.

    The inclusion of Solitaire in Windows from version 3.0 was not just for entertainment; it was intentionally designed to familiarise users with the drag-and-drop mouse operation, serving a dual purpose by teaching computing skills through a simple, engaging game, illustrating Microsoft's strategy of combining utility with user engagement in its software design.

603. The Lemmings' **"Oh no!"** sound clip, played just before a lemming explodes after being assigned the bomber role, became an iconic and darkly humorous element of the game.

604. The **"wololo"** sound from Age of Empires (AoE), used by the Priest unit to convert enemy units, became a meme within the gaming community, applied to situations involving persuasion or change of opinion, transcending its original context to become a universal symbol of conversion or persuasion in internet culture.

    This memorable chant showcased the game's attention to detail and historical references, as it was inspired by the chanting practices of religious figures, illustrating how sound effects in games can enhance immersion and create lasting cultural impacts beyond the gaming world.

605. The phrase **"Job's done"**, announced in a distinctive tone by the human Peasant unit upon completing a task in Blizzard's StarCraft, inadvertently became a catchphrase for players signalling the completion of any real-world chore or task.

    While the iconic "Job's done" notification is closely associated with StarCraft, it originally comes from Warcraft: Orcs & Humans and was prominently used in Warcraft II, and further exemplified by its continued use and recognition in the Hearthstone digital card game.

606. The Command & Conquer (C&C) series is famous for its **unit response sounds**, with units often replying in humorous or exaggerated ways when selected or ordered to move, such as the GDI's Mammoth Tank driver's confident "Rollin'" or the Nod soldier's eager "Yes, sir!" These quirky responses added a layer of personality and humour to the game, endearing the units to players and making each click a little more entertaining.

    The memorable "Acknowledged" response from various units across the C&C series not only became a staple of the game's interaction but also highlighted the game's innovative use of voice-overs to enhance player immersion and feedback. This approach to sound design in strategy games was relatively novel at the time and contributed to setting a higher standard for audio in video games, demonstrating how sound could be used to add depth and character to gameplay.

    The Command & Conquer series is equally renowned for its soundtrack, composed by **Frank Klepacki**, whose fusion of rock, electronic, and industrial themes perfectly encapsulated the game's futuristic and wartime atmosphere. Tracks like "Hell March" from Red Alert became iconic, not just as background music but as integral components of the C&C experience, influencing the way music is used in video games to enhance thematic depth and player immersion.

607. **Carmageddon**, released in 1997, was infamous for its controversial gameplay, which included gaining time and points for running over pedestrians. The exaggerated **screams of the pedestrians** became a darkly humorous and grimly satisfying feedback for players, contributing to the game's notoriety and the debates around video game violence at the time.

Despite (or because of) its controversial nature, Carmageddon's use of pedestrian screams was part of a broader strategy to immerse players in a dystopian world where cars ruled, showcasing the game's innovative approach to open-world design and interactive environments. This level of interactivity, combined with its dark humour, helped Carmageddon stand out in the crowded racing game genre of the 90s.

608. In the classic strategy game **Syndicate**, developed by Bullfrog Productions and released in 1993, selecting agents on the futuristic, cyberpunk-inspired battlefield was accompanied by a distinctive **"selected"** sound. This audio cue became emblematic of the game's tactical depth, with its robotic, slightly echoing quality adding to the atmosphere of controlling cybernetically enhanced agents.

609. The **MP3 format**, officially introduced in 1993, quickly became the de facto standard for digital music due to its ability to compress files significantly while retaining a level of audio quality acceptable to most listeners.

Early MP3 adopters often found themselves on a quest for software capable of playing these files, with Winamp becoming the hero of the hour for many.

610. The act of downloading a single MP3 file could take hours or even an entire night over dial-up internet connections, leading to the widespread practice of starting a download before bed and hoping for a completed song by morning –

Echoes of a Decade: The Quintessential Sounds of 90s PCs

unless someone picked up the phone and disconnected the internet.

611. MP3 files catalysed the creation of peer-to-peer (P2P) file-sharing networks, with Napster being the most infamous.

612. Burning MP3s onto CDs was akin to performing modern alchemy, transforming digital music files into physical media that could be played in the car or on any CD player, marking a transitional phase in music consumption from purely physical to increasingly digital.

613. The proliferation of MP3 files and the ease of sharing them online sparked a major shift in the music industry, challenging traditional business models and copyright laws, and inadvertently turning countless ordinary users into unwitting pirates over their quest for a diverse digital music library.

614. The rise of MP3s and the piracy of games and software during the 90s played a significant role in driving the demand for larger storage capacities on personal computers. As digital media collections grew and software became more complex, users sought out PCs with bigger hard drives to accommodate their expanding libraries of music, games, and applications, accelerating the push for advancements in storage technology and larger standard hard drive sizes in the industry.

THE SYMPHONY OF MODEMS: CONNECTING THE 90S

615. **Baud rates**, representing the transmission speed of modems in bits per second (bps), were a key spec for internet users in the 90s. The journey from 2400 bps to 28.8 Kbps and eventually to 56 Kbps modems marked significant milestones in online speed, with each jump dramatically improving the web browsing experience.

616. The introduction of "v.90" and later "v.92" standards for modems in the late 90s significantly increased the maximum download speeds up to 56 Kbps, marking a pinnacle in dial-up technology before the widespread adoption of broadband.

617. The excitement of upgrading from a 14.4 Kbps modem to a 28.8 Kbps or 56 Kbps modem was akin to moving from a bicycle to a sports car in terms of internet speed, drastically reducing download times and making online gaming and multimedia more accessible.

618. In the early days of the internet, baud rates were a crucial factor in determining which online activities were feasible; lower speeds sufficed for text-based email and browsing, while higher speeds were necessary for downloading files or multimedia content, shaping user habits and expectations around their connection capabilities.

619. Dial-up modems and their baud rates also introduced many to the concept of latency and bandwidth limitations, teaching a generation the virtues of patience and the importance of efficient web design to accommodate slower connections.

620. Configuring a modem for dial-up internet involved manually entering a string of initialisation commands, a process that felt akin to casting a spell to coax the digital spirits into

granting you access to the World Wide Web, showcasing the almost arcane knowledge required to navigate early internet setup.

621. **Configuring network settings** often required toggling between various TCP/IP configurations and proxy settings, a complex dance that underscored the technical barriers to online access and the DIY spirit that characterised early personal computing.

622. The ritual of disconnecting from the internet to free up the phone line is a nostalgic memory for many, symbolising the shared struggles and compromises of household internet access before the advent of always-on broadband connections.

623. Users often accessed dial-up connections through the **"Network Connections"** interface in Windows, where they would set up a new dial-up connection by entering the phone number provided by their ISP, along with their username and password, marking one of the earliest user interactions with network settings in Windows.

624. The "HyperTerminal" application in Windows was used to troubleshoot modem connections, allowing users to directly communicate with the modem using AT commands. This tool was crucial for diagnosing connection issues, such as verifying that the modem could connect to the telephone line and dial out.

625. Internet connection speeds were measured in kilobits per second (Kbps), with 28.8Kbps and 56Kbps modems representing significant milestones in speed improvement, though they now seem laughably slow compared to today's broadband and fibre-optic connections.

626. Windows **Dial-Up Networking (DUN)** provided a wizard for creating and managing dial-up connections, becoming a familiar process for users setting up their internet access. This wizard streamlined the setup process, guiding users

The Symphony of Modems: Connecting the 90s

through the steps of configuring their modem, dial-up number, and login credentials.

627. To optimise their internet experience, users often tweaked settings in the "Internet Options" panel within the Windows Control Panel, adjusting properties like the default dial-up connection, LAN settings, and the browser's cache settings to improve connection speed and performance.

628. The cost of internet access often included both the ISP subscription and the phone company's charges for dial-up time, making unlimited access plans a coveted luxury and leading to late-night internet sessions to take advantage of off-peak rates.

629. The introduction of the **Internet Connection Sharing (ICS)** feature in later versions of Windows allowed multiple devices to share a single dial-up connection, marking an early foray into home networking. This feature required navigating network settings to configure the host computer to serve as a gateway for other devices.

630. **AOL (America Online)** became synonymous with the internet for many in the 90s, known for its all-in-one software that combined internet access, email, and browsing, along with its infamous "You've got mail" greeting, making it a cornerstone of early online experiences.

631. The proliferation of AOL trial CDs, which were mailed to homes and found in magazines, offering hundreds of free hours of internet access, became a cultural phenomenon, often joked about for their abundance and repurposed as coasters or art projects.

632. **Compuserve**, one of the first major commercial ISPs, offered a blend of services including forums, software libraries, and email, targeting professional and business users before becoming more mainstream in the 90s, illustrating the evolution of online services to broader markets.

633. **Prodigy**, launched as a joint venture by IBM and Sears, aimed to create an online service that combined shopping, news, email, and community features, pioneering the concept of an online portal but also facing challenges with its closed system as the World Wide Web opened up.

634. The concept of "unlimited access" plans was revolutionary, with ISPs like EarthLink and NetZero challenging the norm of hourly rates for internet usage, leading to significant shifts in how people accessed and used the internet, encouraging longer sessions and the growth of online content consumption.

635. The "busy signal" when trying to connect to the internet was a common frustration for users, especially during peak hours, highlighting the limitations of infrastructure and the demand for internet access in households sharing a single phone line.

636. Early ISPs often provided personalised web spaces for users to create their own websites, fostering the growth of personal web pages and the DIY spirit of the early web.

637. **Bulletin Board Systems (BBSs)** were the precursor to modern internet forums, where users dialled in directly to another computer over a phone line to post messages, share files, and play games, creating tight-knit online communities before the World Wide Web became mainstream.

638. Many BBSs were run by hobbyists from their own homes, using a personal computer and one or more dedicated phone lines, showcasing the DIY ethos of early online culture and the personal investment of BBS operators in fostering digital communities.

639. BBSs often had unique themes or focuses, ranging from computer programming and gaming to specific hobbies or interests, allowing users to find niche communities where they could share information and forge friendships with like-minded individuals.

The Symphony of Modems: Connecting the 90s

640. Door games, or BBS-based games, such as "Legend of the Red Dragon" (LORD) and "TradeWars 2002," were highly popular, offering multiplayer experiences that kept users coming back daily to continue their adventures, contributing to the early culture of online gaming.

641. The transition to the World Wide Web in the late 90s led to a decline in BBS popularity, but the sense of community and interactive engagement they provided can be seen as a direct ancestor of today's online forums, social media platforms, and multiplayer gaming communities.

642. **Sysops** (System Operators) of BBSs were the unsung heroes of the early internet, dedicating time, resources, and considerable effort to maintain these systems, moderate discussions, and curate content, laying the groundwork for the concept of community management in digital spaces.

643. In the early days of **multiplayer** games, players would connect directly to each other's computers using their modems, a process known as "peer-to-peer" gaming, which required exchanging phone numbers and often enduring the trial and error of establishing a stable connection.

644. Early modem multiplayer required significant patience and technical knowledge, as players often had to configure their own game settings, modem configurations, and sometimes even navigate DOS commands to start a game session.

645. In the early days of modem multiplayer games, players would connect directly to each other's computers using their modems, a process known as "peer-to-peer" gaming, which required exchanging phone numbers and often enduring the trial and error of establishing a stable connection.

646. The sense of community in early modem multiplayer games was strong, with players relying on BBSs and early

The Symphony of Modems: Connecting the 90s

internet forums to find opponents, share strategies, and arrange game times.

647. The phrase **"getting kicked offline"** became part of the 90s internet lexicon, referring to the frustration of losing your internet connection due to a variety of factors, from someone picking up another phone in the house to network congestion, encapsulating the precarious nature of dial-up connectivity.

THE WEB WE WOVE: EARLY NETWORKING

648. During the DOS era, **multiplayer LAN gaming** often required the installation and configuration of Novell NetWare drivers, which were essential for enabling network connectivity on DOS-based systems.

649. Games like **"Doom" (1993)** and **"Duke Nukem 3D" (1996)** popularised LAN multiplayer gaming in the DOS era, requiring players to use command-line instructions to set up and join games, reflecting the hands-on technical knowledge necessary for early network gaming.

650. **IPX/SPX protocol** support was crucial for multiplayer gaming over LANs, with many DOS games requiring this network protocol to communicate between computers.

651. Setting up a LAN for gaming often involved manual configuration of network settings, including IRQs (Interrupt Request Lines) and I/O addresses for network interface cards.

652. The use of batch files to automate the loading of network drivers and game executables streamlined the process of starting a LAN gaming session.

653. The transition from DOS-based networking to Windows brought about a shift in how LAN games were set up and played, with Windows offering a more graphical and user-friendly approach to networking, eventually making the complexities of DOS networking a nostalgic memory for early LAN gamers.

654. **10base2 networks**, also known as "thinnet," utilised coaxial cable and BNC connectors to link computers in a bus topology, a setup that required careful planning and physical layout to ensure connectivity.

655. The process of terminating a 10base2 network involved attaching a terminator to each end of the coaxial cable to prevent signal bounce, a critical step that could lead to hours of troubleshooting if overlooked.

656. The reliance on 10base2 and BNC connectors reflected the state of networking technology and practices in the 90s, where networking was as much a physical endeavour as a digital one, requiring a blend of technical knowledge and practical skill to navigate the limitations and possibilities of early LAN setups.

657. Troubleshooting a 10base2 network often meant walking the length of the coaxial cable to find a loose connection or a missing terminator, a task that could be as frustrating as it was physically demanding, illustrating the challenges of maintaining continuity in a bus topology.

658. The shift to **10base-T and RJ45** connectors made home networking more accessible, as enthusiasts could now more easily expand their networks without the need for precise terminations, simply by plugging in standard ethernet cables, representing a democratisation of network setup and expansion.

659. Crossover cables became a staple for directly connecting two computers without a hub or switch, a useful trick for quick file transfers or gaming between two machines, illustrating the growing sophistication and adaptability of home network configurations.

660. Many enthusiasts learned to crimp their own RJ45 connectors onto CAT5 cable, a skill that became almost a rite of passage. Getting the color-coded wiring correct—adhering to the T568A or T568B standards—was crucial for a successful crimp and a working network connection.

661. The transition also introduced the challenge of choosing the right category of twisted pair cable for the network's speed requirements, with CAT5 being sufficient for 10/100 Mbps networks, and later CAT5e and CAT6 supporting

gigabit speeds, reflecting the increasing demand for faster home internet connections.

662. The introduction of hubs and switches for home use alongside 10base-T technology allowed for more sophisticated home networks with multiple devices, supporting the burgeoning trend of internet-connected homes with shared printers, file storage, and internet access.

663. The practical aspects of building a 10base-T network, such as the need for precise cable management and the ability to diagnose connectivity issues through blinking lights on a hub or switch, underscored the increasingly technical nature of home computing and networking.

664. The adoption of **TCP/IP** as the standard networking protocol simplified the process of connecting computers to the internet and each other, providing a universal communication method that allowed for easier setup and more reliable connections compared to earlier protocols.

665. TCP/IP enabled not just LAN gaming but also internet-based multiplayer gaming, expanding the possibilities beyond local networks to global connectivity.

666. The configuration of TCP/IP settings became more user-friendly over time, with operating systems incorporating automatic IP address assignment via DHCP (Dynamic Host Configuration Protocol), significantly reducing the manual setup required for network connections.

667. Networking parties or **"LAN parties"** in the 90s required participants to physically transport their desktop computers, CRT monitors, and peripherals to a host's location, often resulting in cars filled with bulky equipment for a weekend of gaming.

668. The setup process involved extensive cabling, with ethernet cables running across floors and between rooms,

creating a maze of wires that connected each participant's computer to the network.

669. Network switches and hubs were central to connecting multiple PCs, and troubleshooting connectivity issues was a common group activity, fostering a collaborative problem-solving environment.

670. Power management was crucial, as the combined electrical draw of multiple high-powered PCs and monitors required careful distribution to avoid tripping circuit breakers.

671. Popular genres for LAN party games included FPS and RTS titles that offered engaging multiplayer experiences and became staples of the LAN party scene.

672. All players had to be patched up to the same version of a game for compatibility. Game patches and mods were shared via the network or on floppy disks and CDs, allowing players to synchronise their game versions and try out new content together.

673. Custom maps and levels created by the community added variety and a personal touch to the gaming experience, encouraging creativity and sharing among players.

674. The physical proximity of players at LAN parties facilitated direct communication and teamwork (or sometimes cheating), intensifying the competitive and cooperative aspects of gaming.

675. Snacks, junk food, and caffeinated beverages were LAN party essentials, fuelling marathon gaming sessions that could last for hours or even days if players also took sleeping bags.

676. Sleep was often deprioritised in favour of extended gaming sessions, with players taking turns resting while others continued playing through the night.

677. Setting up a dedicated server on one of the PCs allowed for smoother game performance and centralised control over the gaming session, enhancing the multiplayer experience.

678. Utilising a **dedicated game server** at LAN parties not only enhanced game performance but also allowed the host to tweak session configurations, like adjusting game parameters or map rotations, and even spy on gameplay to commentate or moderate. Games such as "StarCraft" and "Counter-Strike" supported dedicated servers, offering server-side controls that enriched the LAN gaming experience.

679. The end of a LAN party often involved collaborative clean-up efforts, looking for lost items, packing up equipment, and making plans for the next gathering.

680. The camaraderie and shared memories forged at LAN parties left a lasting impact on participants, creating a sense of nostalgia for a time when gaming was as much about community and connection as it was about the games themselves.

681. The decline of LAN parties in favour of online multiplayer gaming marked the end of an era, but the spirit of these gatherings lives on in the memories of those who experienced them and in modern gaming events that strive to recapture the communal atmosphere of 90s LAN parties.

682. The **Wi-Fi** protocol (IEEE 802.11) was officially ratified in 1997, marking the beginning of wireless networking standards that would eventually allow computers to connect to the internet without the need for physical cables.

683. Early Wi-Fi adoption in the late 90s was limited by high costs and low data rates, with the original 802.11 standard supporting speeds of only up to 2 Mbps, a far cry from today's high-speed wireless connections but a revolutionary step forward at the time.

684. The term "Wi-Fi" itself wasn't coined until 1999, with the Wi-Fi Alliance forming to promote wireless technology and certify products as interoperable, helping to ensure that devices could communicate effectively across different manufacturers.

685. Security protocols for Wi-Fi in the 90s were rudimentary by today's standards, with WEP (Wired Equivalent Privacy) being the primary security measure, later revealed to have significant vulnerabilities, highlighting the evolving challenge of securing wireless networks.

686. The late 90s saw a vision of a future where internet connectivity would be ubiquitous and untethered, a concept that seemed almost futuristic at the time but would become a defining characteristic of the 21st century's digital landscape.

VIRTUAL FRONTIERS: WEBSITES AND SERVICES

687. **WebCrawler**, launched in 1994, was one of the first web search engines to index the entire text of web pages, making it a pioneering tool for navigating the burgeoning World Wide Web and setting a standard for future search engines.

688. **Lycos**, also founded in 1994, quickly became a major internet portal and search engine, known for its comprehensive directory of websites and its "Lycos Top 5%" feature highlighting the best of the web, reflecting the era's emphasis on curating quality content.

689. **Yahoo!**, also founded in 1994 as "Jerry and David's Guide to the World Wide Web," quickly evolved from a directory to a full-fledged web portal, offering email, news, and shopping, and becoming synonymous with the internet experience for many in the late 90s.

690. **Excite**, started in 1995, was more than just a search engine; it offered a full internet portal experience with news, weather, email, and a customisable homepage, embodying the 90s trend of portals as gateways to the internet.

691. **AltaVista**, also launched in 1995, was celebrated for its superior search technology, offering fast and relevant search results with advanced search options, and was the first to introduce natural language queries, making it a favourite among tech-savvy users.

692. **Dogpile**, launched in 1996, distinguished itself by aggregating search results from multiple search engines, offering users a more comprehensive overview of the web at a time when no single search engine dominated the landscape.

Virtual Frontiers: Websites and Services

693. **Ask Jeeves** (now Ask.com), founded in 1996, offered a unique approach to search with its focus on natural language queries, inviting users to ask questions as they would to a human, reflecting an early attempt at creating a more interactive and user-friendly search experience.

694. The "I'm Feeling Lucky" button on **Google**, introduced in 1998, directly took users to the top search result, bypassing the results page, a quirky feature that underscored the confidence in Google's search algorithm.

695. The early web was marked by the prominence of "web rings," collections of websites linked together in a circular structure to facilitate navigation among sites with similar themes, a concept supported by search engines and directories to help users discover related content.

696. The rise of **MetaCrawler** in 1995 as a meta-search engine demonstrated the growing need to sift through the rapidly expanding amount of information on the web, aggregating results from several search engines to provide more comprehensive search outcomes.

697. **Northern Light**, launched in 1997, sought to differentiate itself by offering a search engine that catered specifically to the needs of business professionals and researchers, highlighting the diversification of search services to cater to niche audiences.

698. The design and user interface of early search engines were often simple and text-heavy, reflecting the limitations of internet speeds and web technologies of the time, yet their functionality laid the groundwork for the complex algorithms and user interfaces of modern search engines.

699. Early search engines often included manually curated directories of websites, a feature that required significant human effort to maintain and update, illustrating the hands-on approach to organising the web before the advent of automated crawling and indexing.

Virtual Frontiers: Websites and Services

700. The **dot-com bubble** of the late 90s saw massive investments in and acquisitions of search engines and web portals, reflecting the high expectations for the commercial potential of the internet, even as many of these ventures would struggle in the subsequent market correction.

701. Banner ads and sponsored search results began appearing on search engines and portals in the late 90s, marking the early days of online advertising and the monetisation strategies that would become crucial for the sustainability of web services.

702. The decline of several early search engines and portals in the face of competition from more technologically advanced newcomers like Google marked a significant shift in the internet landscape, from the directory and portal model to the dominance of algorithm-driven search engines.

703. **Search bar extensions**, often bundled with free software downloads, became a notorious method of monetisation in the late 90s. These toolbars, once installed, would change a user's default search engine and homepage to drive ad revenue, with Ask Jeeves Toolbar being one of the more recognisable examples.

704. **Pop-up ads** emerged as a prevalent and intrusive form of online advertising, exploiting early web browsers' capabilities to open new windows without user consent. Websites and search engines would use pop-up ads to generate revenue, leading to the development of pop-up blockers as a necessary feature in web browsers.

705. **Adware and spyware** became significant issues, with programs like Gator (later known as Claria) offering to manage passwords and fill out web forms for users while simultaneously tracking their internet usage and displaying targeted ads, blurring the lines between utility and privacy invasion.

706. Browser hijacking software would forcibly redirect users' browsers to specific websites or search engines, dramatically affecting user experience and internet navigation. Examples include **CoolWebSearch**, which redirected users to its own search engine to generate ad revenue.

707. Affiliate marketing programs saw websites earn commissions for referring traffic to online retailers, with **Amazon Associates** being one of the earliest and most successful programs. This encouraged webmasters to create content linking to products, laying the groundwork for many of the monetisation strategies seen on the web today.

708. Early online marketplaces and auction sites, such as eBay, monetised the web by facilitating peer-to-peer sales and transactions, taking a small fee for each sale. This model demonstrated the potential for the internet to revolutionise traditional commerce by connecting buyers and sellers globally.

709. The introduction of paid subscription models for premium content on websites and portals provided an alternative revenue stream beyond advertising, catering to users willing to pay for an ad-free experience or access to exclusive content, a model that continues to be explored and expanded upon by digital media outlets.

710. **Splash screens** on the early web served as digital "welcome mats" for websites, often featuring animated GIFs or Flash animations that loaded before the main content, showcasing web designers' creativity and the novelty of multimedia web content.

711. Notable examples include the animated splash screen for the Space Jam movie website, launched in 1996, which is still live today as a piece of internet history. It features iconic animations and graphics that capture the essence of mid-90s web design.

Virtual Frontiers: Websites and Services

712. Early gaming websites and tech startups frequently used splash screens to build anticipation while the rest of the site loaded, with some splash pages allowing users to choose between a "high bandwidth" or "low bandwidth" version of the site, acknowledging the era's variable internet speeds.

713. The use of splash screens often reflected the limitations of dial-up internet speeds, serving a practical purpose by giving users something to look at while the heavier content of the website loaded in the background, though they sometimes added to the wait time unnecessarily.

714. As web design evolved, splash screens became less common, partly due to improvements in web technologies and faster internet speeds, and partly because of a greater emphasis on user experience design, which prioritised speed and accessibility over flashy entrance pages.

Despite their decline in use, splash screens remain a nostalgic element of the early web for many, symbolising a time when the internet felt like a new frontier to be explored with excitement and a sense of discovery.

715. **GeoCities**, launched in 1994, became a hallmark of early internet culture, offering users free web space to build their own websites, which contributed to the explosion of personal and hobbyist web pages, encapsulating the DIY spirit of the early web.

716. Websites on GeoCities were organised into "neighborhoods" based on their content theme, such as "Area51" for science fiction and fantasy or "Hollywood" for entertainment, creating a sense of community among similarly themed sites.

717. The closure of GeoCities in 2009 led to significant efforts by digital archivists to preserve its content, resulting in the **"GeoCities Archive Project"**, which aimed to save as much of the site's unique cultural footprint as possible, highlighting its significance in internet history.

718. **Angelfire** and **Tripod**, similar to GeoCities, provided free web hosting services and tools for building websites, becoming popular platforms for personal web pages, fan sites, and online diaries, contributing to the vibrant, user-generated web of the late 90s.

719. The aesthetic of GeoCities sites, characterised by tiled backgrounds, animated GIFs, and "under construction" signs, became iconic of the era, symbolising the learning curve and enthusiasm of first-time webmasters navigating web design.

720. Many GeoCities sites featured guestbooks, where visitors could leave comments, predating modern social media interactions and fostering a sense of community and feedback among web users and creators.

721. The reliance on HTML coding, often learned from tutorials shared within the community or from built-in site builders, empowered a generation of web users with the basics of web design and development, laying the groundwork for careers in technology.

722. The popularity of these free web hosting services highlighted the internet's potential as a platform for expression and information sharing, setting the stage for the evolution of blogs, social media, and user-centric content.

723. ISP-provided email accounts, which were common in the 90s, tied users' email addresses to their internet service provider, making email an integral part of the ISP package but also limiting portability, as changing ISPs often meant changing email addresses.

724. **Hotmail**, launched in 1996, was one of the first web-based email services, allowing users to access their emails from any computer with internet access, revolutionising the way people communicated online by not being tied to a single ISP's email service.

Virtual Frontiers: Websites and Services

725. The original spelling of Hotmail was "HoTMaiL," emphasising the HTML within the name to highlight its use of HTML to create a web-based email interface.

726. Hotmail's integration with Windows Live and its eventual transition to Outlook.com marked the end of an era for one of the internet's original email services, reflecting the evolution of digital communication platforms.

727. **Yahoo! Mail**, launched in 1997, quickly became Hotmail's main competitor, offering similar web-based email services with additional features like **Yahoo! Messenger** integration, fuelling the growth of online communication beyond simple email.

728. The concept of **"spam" email** became widely recognised with the growth of email services like Hotmail and Yahoo! Mail, leading to the development of spam filters as an essential feature to protect users from unwanted emails.

729. **Email chains** and early viral content, such as jokes, urban legends, and hoaxes, spread rapidly through services like Hotmail, showcasing the power of email as a tool for sharing content long before the advent of social media.

730. The use of web-based email services for signing up for forums, newsletters, and online accounts became standard practice, underscoring the role of email as a digital identity and gateway to the broader internet.

731. **CNET**, founded in 1994, quickly became a leading source of technology news, product reviews, and software downloads, serving as a crucial resource for tech enthusiasts navigating the rapidly evolving digital landscape of the 90s.

732. One of CNET's early innovations was the launch of **Download.com** in 1996, providing a centralised repository for safe and reliable software, freeware, and shareware downloads, which became indispensable for users looking for a trustworthy source of files.

733. **Slashdot**, launched in 1997 with the slogan "News for Nerds. Stuff that Matters," became famous for its community-driven content and lively discussions, embodying the spirit of the early internet's tech community and serving as a precursor to modern social media platforms.

734. **The Register**, a British technology news and opinion website founded in 1994, gained a reputation for its witty and sometimes irreverent take on tech news, distinguishing itself with a unique voice that appealed to tech professionals and enthusiasts alike.

735. These early tech websites not only provided valuable information but also fostered a sense of community among tech enthusiasts, offering forums and comment sections where readers could engage in discussions, share tips, and offer support long before the advent of social media.

736. **IGN** (Imagine Games Network) was launched in 1996 as a part of the Imagine Media network, quickly becoming a cornerstone for gaming news, reviews, and walkthroughs, setting a high standard for comprehensive coverage of video games across all platforms.

737. **GameSpot**, another early titan in online gaming journalism, was founded in 1996 and became known for its in-depth reviews, industry news, and user forums, offering gamers a reliable source of information and a community for discussion.

738. The early days of IGN featured a unique mix of content beyond traditional game reviews, including cheat codes, strategy guides, and user-submitted reviews, reflecting the interactive and community-driven nature of gaming culture online.

739. **Newgrounds**, founded in 1995, stood apart by focusing on user-generated content, hosting flash games and animations created by its community, showcasing the

Virtual Frontiers: Websites and Services

creative potential of the internet and giving rise to many iconic internet memes and flash games.

740. The rise of these gaming websites coincided with the golden age of PC gaming, providing critical coverage of landmark titles like "Doom," "Half-Life," and "StarCraft," and contributing to the growth of the gaming community by fostering discussion and anticipation for upcoming releases.

741. **Kali** was a pioneering service launched in 1995 that allowed gamers to play online multiplayer games over the internet that were originally designed for LAN play only, effectively simulating a LAN environment across the internet, and bringing games like "Doom" and "Descent" into the early realm of online gaming.

742. The service worked by tricking games into thinking they were operating over a local network, using the IPX protocol, thereby opening up a new world of online gaming possibilities before the widespread adoption of true internet multiplayer capabilities.

743. Kali's user interface included a chat function and a server browser, features that are standard in today's gaming platforms but were innovative at the time.

744. Another service of the era, DWANGO (Dial-up Wide-Area Network Game Operation), provided a similar function by offering a subscription-based service where players could dial into a server to play multiplayer games, highlighting the demand for online multiplayer experiences in the pre-broadband internet era.

745. These services often required a subscription fee, with Kali charging a one-time fee for its software and DWANGO charging monthly access fees, reflecting the premium nature of early online multiplayer gaming.

746. **Leetspeak**, an alternative alphabet used primarily on the internet, emerged in the 1980s but gained significant

popularity in the 90s among hackers, gamers, and the online community as a form of digital insider language. It replaces letters with numbers and symbols that resemble the letters they replace, such as "3" for "E" and "4" for "A" (e.g., "l33t" for "leet" and "h4x0r" for "hacker").

747. Initially, leetspeak was used by hackers to avoid detection by simple text-based search algorithms employed by law enforcement and to demonstrate insider knowledge or skill within the hacker community. For example, using "l33t" instead of "leet" could help evade keyword monitoring.

748. By the late 90s, leetspeak had transcended its origins and become a staple of broader internet culture, particularly in gaming communities and forums where it was used more for playful effect or to signify membership within the digital in-group rather than for its original purpose of evading detection.

749. Leetspeak variations became a form of creative expression, with multiple levels of complexity ranging from simple character substitutions to more elaborate encodings that could include a mix of uppercase and lowercase letters, numbers, and special characters, making the text increasingly difficult to read for those not well-versed in leetspeak.

750. The rise of online multiplayer games in the late 90s further popularised leetspeak, with terms like **"pwned"** (a typographical error for "owned", meaning to defeat or dominate someone) becoming part of the online gaming lexicon, demonstrating how leetspeak contributed to the evolving language of the internet.

751. **"Warez"** refers to pirated software that was widely distributed online during the 90s, often through BBS before moving to early internet forums and IRC channels, becoming a subculture dedicated to the sharing of software, games, and later, movies and music.

Virtual Frontiers: Websites and Services

752. The term "warez" itself is a leetspeak modification of "wares," used to describe software in a way that evaded simple text searches by authorities trying to crack down on illegal file sharing, showcasing the early internet culture's penchant for creative use of language to skirt around legal boundaries.

753. Crack groups, which specialised in removing copy protection from software and games and releasing them to the public, became celebrated within the warez community. Groups like Razor 1911, Fairlight, and SKIDROW gained notoriety for their skills and speed in cracking newly released software.

754. The release of keygens (key generators) and cracks was often accompanied by elaborate ASCII art, chiptune music, and "NFO" files that included instructions, credits to the crackers, and sometimes messages to the software companies or other cracking groups.

755. The practice of **"0-day warez"** referred to the sharing of cracked software on the same day as its official retail release, highlighting the efficiency and competitiveness within the warez community to be the first to crack and distribute new software.

PIXEL PIONEERS: GRAPHICS THAT DEFINED AN ERA

756. **CGA** (Colour Graphics Adapter), introduced by IBM in 1981, was the first colour graphics standard for PCs, capable of displaying up to four colours at 320x200 pixels or two colours at 640x200 pixels, setting the stage for the graphical evolution of personal computers.

   EGA (Enhanced Graphics Adapter) emerged in 1984, offering a significant improvement with 16 colours at a resolution of 640x350, allowing for more detailed images and graphics in both software applications and games, such as "King's Quest" in the 80s which showcased the capabilities of EGA graphics.

757. **VGA** (Video Graphics Array), introduced with the IBM PS/2 line in 1987, became the de facto standard for PC graphics in the 90s, supporting 256 colours from a palette of 262,144 at resolutions up to 640x480, enabling richer and more immersive visual experiences.

758. **SVGA** (Super VGA) was not a standard defined by a single entity but rather a term used to describe any VGA-compatible display system that exceeded VGA's maximum standard resolution, leading to a wide variety of SVGA implementations with different capabilities, often supporting resolutions of 800x600 or higher and a broader colour palette.

759. The introduction of VGA and SVGA standards coincided with the golden age of PC gaming, with titles like **"Doom"**, **"Myst"**, and **"The 7th Guest"** taking full advantage of the enhanced graphics capabilities to deliver visually stunning experiences that were previously unimaginable.

760. **Windows 3.0**, released in 1990, and its successors made extensive use of the capabilities provided by VGA and

SVGA graphics, transforming the user interface of PCs from text-based to graphical, paving the way for the widespread adoption of GUI-based operating systems.

761. The progression from CGA to EGA, and then to VGA/SVGA, mirrored the overall trend in computing towards increasing graphical fidelity and colour depth, reflecting users' growing expectations for more visually rich and engaging content on their PCs.

762. By the mid to late 90s, dedicated **graphics cards** from companies like ATI and NVIDIA began to surpass the capabilities of standard VGA and SVGA integrated graphics, leading to the rise of 3D graphics accelerators which further revolutionised PC gaming and graphics-intensive applications.

763. **3dfx Interactive**, founded in 1994, became synonymous with high-performance 3D graphics in the mid to late 90s, thanks to its revolutionary Voodoo Graphics chipset, which significantly outperformed existing solutions by offloading 3D rendering from the CPU to the GPU.

764. The Voodoo Graphics accelerator, released in 1996, was a game-changer for PC gaming, offering unprecedented 3D graphics quality and performance. It enabled smoother and more immersive experiences in games like **"Descent II"** and **"Need for Speed II"**.

765. 3dfx's **SLI** (Scan-Line Interleave) technology allowed two Voodoo2 cards to be linked together to double the processing power, demonstrating an early use of multi-GPU technology to achieve higher frame rates and resolutions in 3D games, a concept that remains relevant in modern PC gaming.

766. The company's marketing campaigns and branding, with memorable taglines like "3dfx: Because Life is Too Short for Triangles" and the distinctive green colour of its PCBs, helped cement its status as a leader in the burgeoning field of 3D graphics acceleration.

767. Despite its early successes, 3dfx struggled to compete with emerging rivals like NVIDIA and ATI in the late 90s due to delays in product releases and the high cost of its solutions, leading to its eventual acquisition by NVIDIA in 2000, marking the end of an iconic era in PC graphics.

768. Desktop publishing and design software, such as **Adobe Photoshop** and **CorelDRAW**, benefited significantly from the advancements in graphics standards, allowing designers to work with a larger colour palette and higher resolutions, thereby enhancing creativity and productivity.

769. The popularity of **CD-ROM** drives in the 90s, coupled with improved graphics standards, enabled multimedia applications and games to include high-quality images, video, and animations, contributing to the multimedia PC (MPC) standard that defined a new era of content consumption.

770. The competition among graphics chip manufacturers and the rapid advancement of graphics standards in the 90s laid the groundwork for the development of modern GPUs, which are essential for gaming, professional graphics work, and even general computing tasks today.

771. As the 90s progressed, the distinction between professional graphics workstations and consumer PCs began to blur, with high-end PCs capable of graphics and animation work that would have previously required specialised equipment.

772. The end of the 90s saw the beginning of the transition to higher-definition displays and the adoption of digital display interfaces like DVI, setting the stage for the next wave of advancements in display technology and graphics standards in the 2000s.

773. **OpenGL**, introduced by Silicon Graphics in 1992, quickly became the standard for cross-platform, professional 3D graphics programming, enabling developers to create

detailed and complex 3D environments in software ranging from CAD applications to video games.

774. **DirectX** was launched by Microsoft in 1995 to enhance multimedia capabilities on Windows, specifically targeting game development. DirectX aimed to simplify hardware programming for developers and ensure consistent performance across different hardware configurations.

775. The rivalry between OpenGL and DirectX in the 90s mirrored the broader competition between open standards and proprietary technologies, with OpenGL being praised for its cross-platform capabilities and DirectX for its deep integration with the Windows operating system.

776. The release of DirectX 3 in 1996 marked a significant milestone, introducing Direct3D as a competitor to OpenGL for 3D game development on Windows, sparking debates within the developer community about the best platform for 3D graphics programming.

777. OpenGL's adoption by high-end graphics workstation vendors like SGI, and its use in professional visualisation and design applications, contrasted with DirectX's focus on consumer PCs and gaming, highlighting different target markets for each API.

778. The introduction of DirectX 5 and 6 in the late 90s brought significant improvements to the API, including better support for hardware acceleration, which helped solidify DirectX's position as the preferred API for developing Windows games.

779. **"Quake"** was one of the first major games to offer support for both OpenGL and the burgeoning 3D acceleration hardware, showcasing the potential of both APIs for enhancing game graphics and performance.

780. The **"glide"** API, developed by 3dfx for its Voodoo Graphics line of cards, presented a temporary alternative to OpenGL and DirectX, optimised specifically for 3dfx

hardware and offering superior performance in supported titles such as **"Unreal"** before being overshadowed by the broader adoption of DirectX.

781. The late 90s saw the graphics API landscape begin to consolidate around DirectX for Windows gaming, driven by Microsoft's aggressive development and the growing importance of the PC as a gaming platform.

782. OpenGL continued to thrive in professional and academic environments, where its cross-platform nature and robust feature set were crucial, even as DirectX captured the mainstream Windows gaming market.

783. The release of DirectX 7 in 1999 introduced hardware-accelerated transform and lighting (T&L), significantly offloading work from the CPU to the GPU, a feature that would become standard in 3D gaming and graphics applications.

784. The evolution of these APIs throughout the 90s played a critical role in the development of the GPU (Graphics Processing Unit), with hardware manufacturers designing their products to specifically support DirectX and OpenGL standards, influencing the direction of graphics hardware technology.

785. By the end of the 90s, the success of DirectX, particularly in the gaming domain, demonstrated the growing influence of software APIs on hardware development, consumer choices, and the overall trajectory of the graphics industry.

THE BIOS BACKSTORY

786. The **BIOS (Basic Input/Output System)** served as the backbone for PC customisation in the 90s, allowing users to tweak system settings at a hardware level before the operating system loaded.

787. Customising the **boot sequence** in BIOS was a common practice, enabling users to prioritise which devices (hard drive, floppy drive, CD-ROM) the system attempted to boot from first, essential for installations or running diagnostics.

788. Tweaking **memory settings** such as timings and voltages was advanced customisation, allowing users to optimise performance, though it required a careful balance to maintain system stability.

789. **CPU speed and voltage settings** could also be adjusted in the BIOS, a precursor to modern overclocking. Users would increase the clock multiplier and core voltage to boost performance, risking overheating or system failure if pushed too far.

790. **Peripheral configuration** settings in BIOS allowed for the enabling or disabling of onboard components like sound cards, network interfaces, and serial/parallel ports, helping resolve conflicts or free up resources.

791. **Plug-n-Play (PnP) settings** in BIOS helped automatically configure device IRQs and DMA channels, reducing manual setup for peripherals, although it wasn't always seamless and sometimes required manual tweaking.

792. Adjusting **AGP (Accelerated Graphics Port) settings**, including aperture size and data rate, was crucial for optimising graphics card performance, especially for early 3D games and applications.

The BIOS Backstory

793. **PCI (Peripheral Component Interconnect) settings** could be adjusted to specify the IRQ assignments for PCI slots, essential for resolving hardware conflicts in systems with multiple expansion cards.

794. Setting a **BIOS password** was a basic security measure to prevent unauthorised access to the computer's setup utility, protecting against unwanted changes to the system configuration.

795. **IDE Hard Drive Auto Detection** feature allowed the BIOS to automatically recognise and configure new hard drives, simplifying the upgrade process for users.

796. **Shadowing** options were available to copy BIOS routines into faster RAM to speed up system performance, though this had a more noticeable effect on older systems.

797. **BIOS flashing**, the process of updating the BIOS firmware, evolved significantly during the 90s. Initially requiring a bootable floppy disk with the update files, leading to the development of Windows applications that could update the BIOS directly from the operating system, simplifying what was once a risky procedure.

798. The ability to **flash the BIOS** to a newer version from within the BIOS setup itself became more common, allowing users to update their motherboard's firmware to support new hardware and fix bugs.

799. **CMOS Setup** allowed users to save and restore BIOS settings, enabling users to experiment with configurations and easily revert back to a stable setup if necessary.

800. Later, **Windows-based BIOS flashing utilities** like **Award Flash** and **AMI WinFlash** allowed users to update their motherboard's firmware without needing to boot into DOS. These applications lowered the barrier to updating BIOS, making it more accessible for the average user to improve compatibility or add new features to their systems.

The BIOS Backstory

801. The introduction of **dual BIOS technology** towards the late 90s provided a safety net for BIOS flashing, where a backup BIOS chip could restore the system if the update process failed. This innovation also significantly reduced the risk associated with BIOS updates.

802. BIOS setup utilities began to incorporate **graphical interfaces** towards the late 90s, making them more user-friendly and easier to navigate compared to the text-only interfaces of earlier versions.

803. **Power management settings** allowed users to configure power-saving features such as suspend mode and wake-on-LAN functionality, reflecting early efforts to make PCs more energy-efficient.

804. **Energy Star compliance** displayed during the BIOS startup sequence indicated that the PC met specific energy efficiency guidelines set by the U.S. Environmental Protection Agency. This certification meant that the computer was designed to consume less power, especially in standby or off modes, contributing to lower energy bills and reduced environmental impact.

805. BIOS options related to **Energy Star compliance** often included settings for power management, allowing users to configure their systems to automatically power down hard drives or enter sleep mode after periods of inactivity, further enhancing energy efficiency.

806. The push for **Energy Star compliance** also drove the development of more power-efficient components and system designs throughout the 90s, as manufacturers aimed to meet these standards without sacrificing performance, marking an early industry-wide effort towards greener computing solutions.

807. **Temperature monitoring** and **fan speed control** settings started appearing in late 90s BIOS versions, giving users early tools for thermal management in their systems.

The BIOS Backstory

808. **System Health Monitoring** features provided real-time data on CPU temperature, fan speeds, and voltage levels, crucial for overclocking and system stability.

809. A **Quick Boot** feature was introduced to skip certain POST (Power-On Self Test) checks for a faster startup, beneficial for users who rebooted frequently.

810. **Boot from LAN** or **Network Boot** options emerged, allowing computers to load an operating system from a network server, paving the way for diskless workstations and simplified management of multiple PCs.

811. The customisation of **sound alert codes** in BIOS for troubleshooting hardware issues, where different beep patterns would indicate specific problems at startup, helping diagnose issues without a display.

812. **Early 90s Motherboards** relied heavily on jumpers and DIP switches for configuring crucial settings such as the CPU clock speed, voltage, and the system bus speed. These physical configurations required users to manually adjust settings by changing the position of jumpers on the motherboard, a process that was not only time-consuming but also prone to errors.

813. The **mid to late 90s** saw the introduction of **soft BIOS setup utilities** allowed users to configure hardware settings through a graphical or text-based interface. This development significantly simplified the process, enabling changes to be made without opening the case or physically altering the motherboard.

814. By the mid-90s, many BIOS setup programs included options to adjust **processor and memory** timings, voltages, and speeds, functionalities that previously required jumper adjustments. This facilitated overclocking and system tuning directly from the BIOS setup, making it accessible to a broader audience.

815. **Legacy Support**: Despite these advancements, some motherboards continued to use jumpers for critical functions into the late 90s, though this practice became increasingly rare. Manufacturers often provided legacy support for older components that required specific configurations not supported by the BIOS.

PLUGGING IN: THE PORTS OF YESTERYEAR

816. Circular **PS/2 ports**, introduced with the IBM Personal System/2 in 1987, were the standard for connecting keyboards and mice entering the 90s. Their dedicated nature allowed for more efficient input device connections compared to serial ports.

817. **Serial ports** became essential for connecting mice, modems, and other peripherals in the early 90s. Their use for dial-up internet connections made them indispensable for accessing the World Wide Web before the prevalence of Ethernet and Wi-Fi.

818. **Parallel ports**, commonly used for connecting printers, were a standard feature on PCs throughout the 90s. The ability to also connect zip drives and other storage devices via parallel ports later on showcased their versatility.

819. **Plug and Play (PnP)** technology, introduced with Windows 95, aimed to simplify the configuration of peripherals by allowing the operating system to automatically recognise and configure hardware, marking a significant shift towards user-friendly PC configurations.

820. **USB (Universal Serial Bus)**, introduced in 1996, revolutionised peripheral connectivity with its support for hot-swapping, ease of use, and ability to connect multiple devices through a single port. Though slow to be adopted, by the late 90s, USB began to replace serial and parallel ports on new computers.

821. **FireWire (IEEE 1394)**, introduced by Apple in 1995 and adopted by PCs shortly after, offered high-speed data transfer rates ideal for digital video cameras and external hard drives, complementing USB by targeting more bandwidth-intensive applications.

Plugging In: The Ports of Yesteryear

822. **SCSI (Small Computer System Interface)** ports offered a faster alternative to parallel and serial ports for connecting high-speed devices like scanners and hard drives, particularly valued by business and professional users for their performance before USB became widespread.

823. **Ethernet ports (RJ-45)** became common on PCs in the mid to late 90s, facilitating faster and more reliable internet connections compared to dial-up modems. The shift towards broadband internet connections accelerated the adoption of integrated Ethernet in personal computers.

824. **Game ports (DA-15)**, used for connecting joysticks and game controllers, were a staple on sound cards before being phased out in favour of USB. The Sound Blaster series of sound cards was well-known for including game ports.

825. **Infrared (IR) ports** appeared on some laptops and desktops in the mid-90s, allowing for wireless data transfer between computers and early smartphones or PDAs, although they were limited by slow transfer speeds and line-of-sight requirements.

826. The introduction of the **VGA port** standard in 1987 brought higher resolution and colour depth to monitors, becoming the default video connection for PCs.

827. The transition to **digital display interfaces**, with **DVI (Digital Visual Interface)** being introduced in 1999, began to replace VGA for connecting monitors, offering clearer and more stable video quality, although VGA remained ubiquitous for many years after.

828. By the late 1990s, the evolution of external PC ports was marked by a shift from traditional PS/2, serial, and parallel ports to more versatile interfaces like USB and FireWire. This transition catered to the growing demand for easier device management, faster data transfers, and expanded connectivity, paving the way for USB to become the universal standard for connecting peripherals.

PERIPHERALS OF THE PAST

829. **Dot matrix printers** were ubiquitous for home and office use, known for their distinctive printing sound and the ability to print multi-part forms through carbon copies.

830. **Inkjet printers** became popular in the 90s for their ability to print in colour, with brands like HP, Epson, and Canon leading the market. Canon's BubbleJet was especially notable for its compact size and print quality.

831. **Ball mice** dominated the decade, requiring frequent cleaning of the internal rollers to maintain smooth cursor movement due to the accumulation of dust and sweat.

832. **Middle mouse buttons** became a standard feature on many mice in the 90s, offering additional functionality such as opening links in new browser tabs or panning in CAD applications. The Logitech MouseMan, introduced in the early 90s, was among the first to popularise the inclusion of a middle button, enhancing productivity and user interface navigation.

833. **Optical mice**, introduced in the late 90s, began replacing ball mice, offering more precise tracking and eliminating the need for cleaning.

834. **Scroll Wheels** were introduced in the late 90s, simplifying how users navigated through documents and web pages. The Microsoft IntelliMouse, released in 1996, was one of the first to feature a scroll wheel, quickly becoming a must-have feature for mice due to the convenience and efficiency it brought to scrolling through content.

835. **Trackballs** such as the **Logitech TrackMan Marble** offered an alternative to traditional mice, particularly favoured by graphic designers for their precision and by users with limited desk space.

836. **Pointing Sticks**, often called "nipple" mice, were integrated into laptop keyboards, notably on IBM ThinkPads, allowing for mouse control without moving one's hands away from the keyboard.

837. The **IBM Model M Keyboard**, introduced in the mid-80s but widely used through the 90s, became iconic for its durable build and tactile buckling spring key switches, making it a favourite among typists and PC enthusiasts. Other notable keyboards of the 90s included:

    - **Apple Extended Keyboard II (1990)**: Praised for its solid build and satisfying key feel, this keyboard was a favourite among Macintosh users, offering both ADB (Apple Desktop Bus) connections and adjustable legs for comfort.

    - **Microsoft Natural Keyboard (1994)**: Introduced ergonomic design to the masses, featuring a split layout to encourage a more natural hand, wrist, and forearm position. Its distinctive wave shape and separate numeric keypad became iconic.

    - **IBM ThinkPad 701 Butterfly Keyboard (1995)**: Known for its unique expanding mechanism designed for IBM's compact ThinkPad 701 laptop. This innovative keyboard would "butterfly" open as the laptop lid was lifted, allowing for a full-sized keyboard in a smaller form factor.

    - **Compaq Enhanced Keyboard**: Accompanied many Compaq PCs, noted for its sturdy build and comfortable typing experience. It was a common sight in both homes and offices, contributing to Compaq's reputation for quality computer accessories.

    - **Dell QuietKey Keyboard**: Popular in office environments for its affordability and decent key feel. Dell's QuietKey keyboards were widely used in businesses and schools, known for their reliability and quiet typing experience.

Peripherals of the Past

- **Logitech G15 Gaming Keyboard (late 90s)**: Although more associated with the early 2000s, Logitech's entry into gaming keyboards began in the late 90s. The G15, known for its programmable keys and built-in LCD screen, laid the groundwork for future gaming-oriented keyboards.

838. **Joysticks** were essential for PC gaming, especially for flight simulators and arcade-style games. Products like the Microsoft Sidewinder were popular for their ergonomics and programmable buttons.

839. **Flight Sticks** took the joystick concept further, offering more buttons, hat switches, and often throttle controls, enhancing the realism in flight simulation games.

840. **Force Feedback Technology**, introduced in joysticks and steering wheels, added physical resistance to simulate real-world sensations, such as the Microsoft Sidewinder Force Feedback Pro, enhancing immersion in games.

841. **Dongles** were used as a form of copy protection for expensive software such as AutoCAD, LightWave 3D, and Mathematica, plugging into a parallel or serial port, ensuring that the software couldn't run without the corresponding hardware key.

842. **Webcams**, though of low resolution by today's standards, began to become popular for video chatting. Logitech and Creative were early leaders in this market.

843. Early **Digital Cameras** started connecting to PCs via serial or USB ports, allowing users to download photos directly to their computers for editing or sharing online, one example being the Apple QuickTake 100.

844. **Docking Stations** became essential for laptop users needing to connect multiple peripherals, essentially transforming their laptops into desktop PCs with one easy connection.

Peripherals of the Past

845. **External Modems**, initially dominating with dial-up speeds, were crucial for internet access until internal or software-based modems became standard in PCs.

846. **PC Speakers** evolved from simple beeps to full stereo systems with subwoofers, like the Altec Lansing ACS series, catering to the growing demand for high-quality audio for gaming and multimedia.

847. **Scanners**, both flatbed and handheld, became common for home offices, allowing users to digitise documents and photos.

848. **Zip Drives** from Iomega offered a higher-capacity alternative to floppy disks, becoming a popular solution for backups and large file transfers.

849. **Gamepads** began to supplement traditional keyboard and mouse controls for certain games, with the Gravis GamePad being one of the first to gain popularity among PC gamers.

850. **Graphics Tablets**, such as those from Wacom, provided artists and designers with a more natural input method for digital art and photo editing, distinguishing themselves from mice and trackballs for precision work.

851. **VR Headsets**, though rudimentary by today's standards, like the Forte VFX1, gave a glimpse into virtual reality gaming, even if the technology wasn't quite ready for mainstream adoption.

ICONIC TECH BRANDS

852. **3dfx Interactive** revolutionised PC gaming with the Voodoo Graphics Accelerator card, introducing many to 3D graphics and making games like Tomb Raider and Quake phenomenally better.

853. **Abit**, known for its high-performance motherboards, faced financial difficulties and eventually ceased operation.

854. **Adaptec** was synonymous with SCSI host adapters, enabling high-speed peripheral connections with products like the Adaptec AHA-2940 series.

855. **Ambra Computer Corporation**, a short-lived IBM subsidiary, offered budget-friendly PCs such as the Ambra Achiever, targeting home users and small businesses.

856. **Antec** gained recognition for its PC cases and power supplies, with products like the Antec SX1030B case becoming a favourite for its build quality and cooling efficiency.

857. **ATi**, before being acquired by AMD, made waves with the Rage series, particularly the ATi Rage Pro, which was a common choice for OEMs and offered competitive 2D and 3D graphics.

858. **Aureal Semiconductor**, known for its Vortex sound cards, provided innovative audio solutions with 3D sound technology before being acquired by Creative Technology.

859. **Belkin** became synonymous with a wide range of PC cables and accessories, offering reliable connectivity solutions for all sorts of peripherals.

860. **BFG Technologies**, once a manufacturer of NVIDIA graphics cards and power supplies, ceased operations in 2010.

Iconic Tech Brands

861. **Boston Acoustics** made waves in the PC speaker market with the BA635 speaker system, providing exceptional sound quality for desktop users.

862. **Chieftec** made durable and user-friendly PC cases, with the Dragon series being particularly popular for their spacious design and good airflow.

863. **Compaq** was known for the Presario desktops and laptops, offering good performance and value, with the Compaq Presario 425 and 433 being early successes.

864. **Cyrix** made its mark with the 6x86 processors, offering a budget-friendly alternative for PC builders looking for performance without the Intel price tag.

865. **D-Link** was essential in the networking realm with products like the DFE-530TX NIC, offering easy and affordable network access.

866. **Dell** made a name for itself with direct sales of custom-configured PCs, with the Dell Dimension XPS being one of the high-performance models coveted by gamers.

867. **Diamond Multimedia** expanded beyond graphics to modems with the SupraExpress 56k modem, a popular choice for dial-up internet users. They were also a key player in sound with the Diamond Monster Sound card series.

868. **Ensoniq**: Known for their AudioPCI sound cards, which offered a great mix of quality, compatibility, and affordability.

869. **Epox**, recognised for its motherboards catering to the enthusiast market, has faded from the mainstream PC components market.

870. **Gateway 2000** famously shipped PCs in cow-spotted boxes, a nod to their Iowa roots, with products like the Gateway 2000 4DX2-66V being popular home computers.

871. **Guillemot Corporation**, which operated under the Hercules brand for its graphics cards, shifted focus away from the PC hardware market.

872. **Hayes**, the company synonymous with the development of the modem and standards for communication, played a critical role in the early days of internet connectivity before declaring bankruptcy.

873. **Hewlett-Packard (HP)** ventured deeper into personal computing with systems like the HP Vectra PCs, which were known for their reliability and enterprise features.

874. **IBM** created the Aptiva series, known for their innovative designs and multimedia capabilities, making PCs like the IBM Aptiva Stealth a household name.

875. **Iiyama** earned a reputation for high-quality CRT monitors, such as the Vision Master Pro series, offering superior image quality and resolutions for gamers and professionals.

876. **Iomega** became a household name with its Zip drive, a high-capacity floppy disk alternative, offering a solution for data storage and transfer needs before being overtaken by USB flash drives and cloud storage.

877. **Kingston Technology** became a go-to for memory upgrades with its reliable RAM modules, critical for boosting PC performance.

878. **Klipsch** entered the PC market with the ProMedia 2.1 speaker system, setting a high bar for desktop audio performance.

879. **Lian Li** became known for their high-quality aluminium PC cases, like the PC-60, introduced in the late '90s, which was favoured for its craftsmanship, lightweight design, and superior cooling capabilities, setting a standard for luxury computer cases.

Iconic Tech Brands

880. **Matrox** was celebrated for its graphics cards, particularly the Matrox Millennium series, which were known for their sharp 2D graphics quality and stability in professional environments.

881. **Miro Computer Products AG** was notable for its video editing and graphics cards but eventually became part of Pinnacle Systems.

882. **MITSUMI** was known for its floppy drives and keyboards, essential components for PCs during the early to mid-90s.

883. **NEC** was a significant player with its Multisync monitors, which set the standard for high-resolution displays, indispensable for graphic designers and gamers.

884. **Netgear** emerged as a significant player in network interface cards (NICs) with the FA310TX, facilitating fast and reliable wired network connections.

885. **Number Nine Visual Technology** was a pioneer in graphics card technology, introducing innovations with their Imagine series, but eventually faded from the market.

886. **Olivetti**, an Italian company, produced the Olivetti M24, a PC that was advanced for its time, featuring Intel's 8086 microprocessor.

887. **Orchid Technology** was known for its Righteous 3D card, which was among the first to support 3dfx's Glide API, enhancing gaming visuals dramatically.

888. **Packard Bell**, once a major player in the home PC market, sold memorable models like the Packard Bell Legend Series which were staples in many homes.

889. **Panaflo/NMB** fans became the go-to for quiet and efficient cooling, a favourite among PC builders looking to reduce noise while maintaining airflow.

890. **PC Power & Cooling** set the standard for high-quality, reliable power supplies with the Turbo-Cool series, becoming a must-have for high-end builds.

891. **Plextor** also became known for its unbeatable quality in CD-ROM and CD-RW drives, with the PlexWriter series being coveted for its reliability and speed in burning CDs.

892. **Rendition** was a company that produced Verité graphics chipsets, offering competition to early 3D accelerators before fading out of the graphics card market.

893. **S3 Graphics'** ViRGE series was one of the early attempts at integrating 2D/3D acceleration, aiming at the burgeoning gaming market.

894. **Sigma Designs** made a name with their Hollywood Plus MPEG decoder card, enhancing DVD playback on PCs before hardware acceleration became standard.

895. **Soltek**, a manufacturer of motherboards and other computer components, ceased its operations in the mid-2000s.

896. **TEAC** was a go-to for reliable CD-ROM drives, with the TEAC CD-55A being a common sight in many PCs for its durability and compatibility.

897. **Thermalright** began making its mark in the late '90s with high-quality heatsinks that would become essential for overclocking and high-performance builds.

898. **Toshiba** was a leading laptop manufacturer with the Satellite series, offering portable computing solutions with models like the Satellite 2100CDS being popular among mobile professionals.

899. **Turtle Beach** offered a range of sound cards, with the Montego series standing out for delivering high-quality audio to gamers and audio enthusiasts.

Iconic Tech Brands

900. **U.S. Robotics** dominated the modem market with the Sportster series, crucial for connecting users to the burgeoning Internet.

901. **ViewSonic** offered a range of CRT monitors that were beloved by gamers and professionals alike, with the P95f+ model being notable for its crisp images and vibrant colours.

902. **Viglen** was known for its presence in the UK educational sector, often seen in schools with models like the Viglen Dossier NS and Viglen Genie PC.

903. **Yamaha**: Their sound cards, particularly the YMF series, were highly regarded for their superior sound quality and MIDI capabilities.

904. **Zalman** started to make its name towards the end of the '90s with innovative cooling solutions, including their CNPS (Computer Noise Prevention System) line of quiet CPU coolers.

905. **Zoom Telephonics** was another key player in the modem space with the Zoom/Modem V.92 External Modem, offering fast and reliable connections.

EXPANSION QUEST: STANDARDS OF THE 90S

906. **ISA slots** dominated early '90s motherboards for expansion cards, with users commonly inserting sound cards like the Sound Blaster 16 and network cards.

907. **Intel's 486 series** motherboards introduced a variety of CPU sockets and slots, with the Socket 3 being particularly popular for its support of a wide range of 486 processors.

908. **VLB (VESA Local Bus)** offered a significant performance boost for video and hard disk controllers on 486 motherboards but was quickly superseded by newer technologies as Pentium processors became prevalent.

909. **PCI (Peripheral Component Interconnect) slots** improved expansion capabilities over ISA with higher data transfer rates, becoming a standard for devices like the 3Com EtherLink III network card and Matrox Millennium graphics cards.

910. **AGP (Accelerated Graphics Port)** was introduced in 1997, specifically designed to assist 3D graphics processing, marking a significant leap forward for gaming and professional graphics with cards like the NVIDIA RIVA TNT.

911. **SIMM (Single Inline Memory Module)** RAM slots were initially the norm, but by the mid-'90s, **DIMM (Dual Inline Memory Module)** slots began to replace them, allowing for faster and larger RAM installations.

912. **EDO (Extended Data Output)** RAM emerged as an improvement over traditional FPM (Fast Page Mode) RAM, reducing the time between memory reads and significantly boosting the performance of systems, particularly with Intel

Pentium and compatible CPUs. EDO RAM became a standard choice in mid-90s PCs.

913. **The AT motherboard form factor** was common at the decade's start but was gradually replaced by the **ATX form factor,** introduced by Intel in 1995, which offered improved layout and power management features.

914. **The Baby AT form factor**, a smaller version of the AT form factor, was widely used throughout the early to mid-'90s for desktop computers, designed to fit into more compact cases while still providing support for a full range of expansion slots and ports. As the decade progressed, it was gradually supplanted by the ATX and Baby ATX (also known as Mini-ATX) standards, which offered improved layout, better air flow, and easier access to motherboard components.

915. **Socket 7** became a universal socket accepting various CPUs, including Intel Pentium, AMD K6, and Cyrix 6x86, allowing for greater compatibility and flexibility in CPU choice.

916. The introduction of the **Pentium** Pro and its unique **Socket 8** in the mid-'90s highlighted the move towards specialised sockets for high-end processors, catering to servers and workstations.

917. **Ultra DMA (Direct Memory Access) IDE interfaces** appeared on motherboards late in the decade, significantly speeding up hard drive data transfer rates and supporting the faster hard drives of the time, like the Quantum Fireball.

918. The rise of onboard components, such as audio and network controllers, began to reduce the need for certain types of expansion cards, a trend that would continue into the next century.

919. **SCSI (Small Computer System Interface)** support was only featured on high-end motherboards for connecting

multiple devices like hard drives and scanners, catering to power users and professionals with boards like those from Adaptec.

920. **Slot 1** and **Slot A** were introduced by Intel and AMD, respectively, for their high-end CPUs, moving away from socket-based installations and symbolising the intense competition between the two.

921. The first motherboards with **USB (Universal Serial Bus)** support emerged before the end of the decade, heralding a new era of connectivity that would eventually standardise peripheral connections.

922. **ZIF (Zero Insertion Force) sockets** became standard for CPU installations by the mid-'90s, greatly simplifying the process of installing or upgrading processors without the need for excessive force, with popular examples including the Intel Socket 7 and the later Socket 370, accommodating a wide range of CPUs from the Pentium to the Pentium III series.

923. **Intel 440BX chipset**, introduced in 1998, became one of the most beloved chipsets for Pentium II and III processors, offering excellent stability and performance, along with support for AGP 2x graphics cards and SDRAM.

924. **VIA Apollo VP3** was a popular chipset for Socket 7 CPUs, known for its support of both SDRAM and EDO RAM, making it a favourite among budget-conscious builders aiming for high performance with AMD and Cyrix processors.

925. **Intel 810 chipset**, also known as the "Whitney" chipset, marked Intel's foray into integrated graphics, providing a cost-effective solution for entry-level PCs without the need for an additional graphics card.

926. **Dual CPU motherboards** like the Tyan S1832DL Tiger 100 and the ASUS P2B-DS became popular in high-end workstations and servers, offering parallel processing

Expansion Quest: Standards of the 90s

capabilities with two Pentium II or Pentium III processors for significantly improved computing power.

927. **ECC RAM (Error-Correcting Code Random Access Memory)** was highly valued in servers and workstations for its ability to detect and correct minor data corruption, ensuring data integrity and system stability in critical applications. While more expensive and slightly slower than non-ECC RAM, its use was essential in high-end computing environments where reliability was paramount, particularly with motherboards designed to support Intel Xeon processors.

928. **The introduction of the Intel Xeon processor** in 1998 brought about the need for specialised motherboards with Slot 2, designed to accommodate these higher-end CPUs aimed at servers and workstations, featuring support for larger caches and ECC (Error-Correcting Code) memory.

929. **SiS 6326 chipset** was known for its integrated graphics capabilities, offering a low-cost solution for motherboards without the need for a separate graphics card, though it was more common in the budget PC market.

930. **AMD 750 chipset** marked AMD's entrance into the chipset market to support their Athlon processors, providing a platform optimised for 3D graphics and high-speed memory, and it was crucial for AMD's competitiveness against Intel.

931. **The ABIT BP6** was one of the first motherboards designed to support dual Celeron processors with Socket 370, making dual-CPU configurations accessible to enthusiasts and power users on a budget.

932. **Intel's 440LX chipset**, introduced in 1997, was designed for the early Pentium II processors, supporting AGP 1x graphics and SDRAM, paving the way for future chipset innovations.

933. **The rise of the Slot 1 and Socket 370** allowed for the broader adoption of Intel's Celeron and Pentium III processors, with motherboards designed around these formats enabling a wide range of performance and budget options for consumers.

934. **Slot 2** motherboards and CPUs – introduced by Intel as a higher-end companion to Slot 1, specifically designed to accommodate the larger physical package of the Pentium II Xeon and Pentium III Xeon processors – supported advanced features like larger cache sizes and dual-processor configurations, catering to the needs of high-performance computing environments in the late 90s.

FADED FUTURES: THE TECH THAT TIME FORGOT

935. **MCA (Micro Channel Architecture)**, introduced by IBM in the late 80s, was intended to replace ISA but struggled due to its proprietary nature and high licensing costs, limiting its adoption primarily to IBM PS/2 computers.

936. **EISA (Extended Industry Standard Architecture)** was developed as an answer to MCA's proprietary issues, offering a 32-bit bus in response to the 16-bit ISA bus. Despite this, EISA was overshadowed by the cheaper and faster VLB and PCI standards.

937. **Cyrix processors**, known for their 6x86 series, offered a budget alternative to Intel's Pentium processors but suffered from compatibility issues and performance inconsistencies, eventually leading to the company's decline.

938. **RISC (Reduced Instruction Set Computer) processors** in personal computers, such as those by MIPS and DEC, aimed to offer higher efficiency but struggled to gain widespread adoption in the PC market dominated by CISC architectures like Intel's x86.

939. The **PowerPC** alliance between Apple, IBM, and Motorola faced challenges in the PC market, despite the chips' superior performance in some benchmarks compared to Intel's offerings. The lack of Windows compatibility and the smaller ecosystem of software available for PowerPC-based systems, like the Apple Power Macintosh, led to difficulties in gaining a foothold outside of niche markets and eventually contributed to Apple's shift to Intel processors in the 2000s.

940. The term **"information superhighway"** was widely used in the early '90s to describe the potential of the internet and

broadband networks but eventually fell out of favour for simpler terms like "the internet."

941. **Gopher**, a text-based protocol intended for distributing, searching, and retrieving documents over the internet, was overshadowed by the World Wide Web's graphical interface and hyperlink capabilities.

942. **The word "weblog"** emerged in the late '90s to describe online journals or diaries; it was eventually shortened to "blog," becoming a mainstream term in the 2000s.

943. **"Netizen"**, a portmanteau of "internet" and "citizen", was used to describe individuals actively involved in online communities but is less commonly used today.

944. **Microsoft Bob** was an early attempt at creating a user-friendly interface for Windows, featuring a cartoonish, room-themed UI; it was widely criticised for its oversimplification and quickly discontinued.

945. **Clippy**, the animated paperclip assistant in Microsoft Office, became infamous for its intrusive help suggestions, leading to its removal in later versions due to user annoyance.

946. **The HTML <marquee> tag** allowed text to scroll across the screen on web pages, widely used in the early days of web design but criticised for its distracting nature and eventually deprecated in HTML standards.

947. **The <blink> tag**, introduced by Netscape, caused text to blink on and off, quickly becoming infamous for its distracting and often headache-inducing effect on web pages before being deprecated due to widespread disdain and lack of support in other browsers.

948. **The <bgsound> tag**, specific to Internet Explorer, allowed background sound to play on a web page but was widely criticised for being intrusive and annoying, leading to its

Faded Futures: The Tech that Time Forgot

eventual deprecation in favour of user-controlled media playback elements.

949. **The Logitech Cyberman**, an early attempt at a 3D controller for PCs, promised a new level of interaction with games but failed to gain widespread acceptance due to limited software support and awkward ergonomics.

950. **IBM's Warp OS/2**, intended as a competitor to Windows, offered robust multitasking capabilities but struggled to win over consumers and developers, eventually fading into obscurity.

951. **The Iomega Zip drive**, while initially popular for its higher storage capacity compared to floppy disks, fell away due to the rise of CD-RW drives and USB flash drives offering even greater storage and convenience.

952. **BiTronics parallel port technology**, despite its improvements in bidirectional data transfer for printers and scanners, was quickly overshadowed by the faster and more versatile USB standard.

953. **ATI's Rage Fury MAXX graphics card**, featuring dual GPUs, struggled with driver issues and compatibility problems, failing to compete effectively against NVIDIA's more powerful and efficient single-GPU solutions.

954. **The 2D/3D graphics accelerator cards by Rendition**, such as the Verite series, were initially popular for their performance but failed to keep pace with the rapid advancements made by competitors like 3dfx and NVIDIA.

955. **WaveTable synthesis for PC sound cards**, offering higher quality MIDI music by storing instrument sounds in ROM, became less critical as digital audio playback capabilities (MP3 and CD audio) became the primary focus for users.

956. **The Advanced Graphics Port (AGP) Pro slot**, designed for high-end graphics workstations with additional power

requirements, saw limited use as the industry quickly moved towards more versatile PCIe slots.

957. **Intel's i740 graphics chipset**, Intel's attempt to enter the graphics market, failed to compete against established players due to its mediocre performance and the rapid evolution of 3D graphics technology.

958. **The IBM PCjr**, intended to be a home computer that could run PC-compatible software, was criticised for its high cost, poor keyboard design, and limited expandability, leading to its market failure.

959. **The Borland Office for Windows**, despite Borland's success with software development tools, struggled to compete against Microsoft Office due to compatibility issues and a lack of market presence, resulting in poor sales.

960. **The Gateway Destination**, an early attempt at a home theatre PC, combined a PC with a large CRT monitor intended for living room entertainment but failed due to its high price and the complexity of integrating it with other home entertainment components.

961. **Intel's Pentium III 1.13 GHz processor** was quickly recalled after its launch due to stability issues at its rated speed, tarnishing Intel's reputation and allowing competitors like AMD to gain market share.

962. **The eWorld online service by Apple**, launched in 1994 as a competitor to AOL and other internet service providers, suffered from high access costs and limited content, leading to its closure within two years.

963. **The NEC UltraLite**, considered one of the first ultraportable laptops, was innovative but its high price and limited performance compared to full-size laptops led to poor sales.

Faded Futures: The Tech that Time Forgot

964. **The Packard Bell Corner Computer**, designed to save space by fitting into the corner of a room, was a unique concept but didn't catch on due to its odd shape and the limitations this design placed on expansion and usability.

965. **Orchid Righteous 3D**, despite being one of the first 3D graphics accelerators for PCs and offering impressive performance at the time, was quickly surpassed by more advanced and versatile graphics solutions from 3dfx and NVIDIA.

966. The **Magellan** Explorer replacement for Windows Explorer, offered advanced file management features but failed to gain significant traction due to Windows users' familiarity with and preference for the built-in file manager.

967. **Daikatana**, developed by Ion Storm and led by John Romero, became infamous for its delayed release, underwhelming gameplay, and failed to live up to the massive hype generated by its marketing campaign, which promised a revolutionary first-person shooter experience.

968. **Battlecruiser 3000AD**, released by 3000AD, Inc., faced a tumultuous development cycle and was notorious for its bugs and steep learning curve upon its initial release, leading to negative reviews and customer dissatisfaction despite its ambitious open-world gameplay.

969. Lionhead Studios' **"Black & White"**, while not a complete failure, faced criticism for failing to fully deliver on its ambitious promise of a god game with an adaptive AI that learns from player interaction, leading to mixed reviews.

970. **SiN Episodes**, developed by Ritual Entertainment, was planned as an episodic series for the first-person shooter genre but was discontinued after just one episode due to poor sales and mixed reviews, showcasing the risks of episodic game development.

971. **"Outpost"** by Sierra On-Line was released with great expectations as a space colony management sim but was

criticised for missing features, bugs, and incomplete gameplay mechanics, leading to disappointment and poor sales.

972. Apogee Software's **"Rise of the Triad: Dark War"**, while having a cult following, was overshadowed by other shooters of its time like "Doom" and "Quake" due to its dated engine and quirky design choices, limiting its impact on the first-person shooter market.

973. Interplay's **"Descent to Undermountain"** attempted to blend the popular Descent engine with Dungeons & Dragons role-playing elements but was marred by bugs, poor controls, and lacklustre gameplay, leading to negative reviews and disappointed fans.

974. **"Extreme Paintbrawl"**, a paintball shooting game, was rushed to market with minimal development time, resulting in a game plagued by poor AI, lack of game modes, and unrealistic physics, earning it a place among the worst-reviewed games of its era.

975. **"Trespasser**, a 1998 game sequel to The Lost World: Jurassic Park, intended to rejuvenate the action-adventure genre with its physics-based gameplay and complex AI, ended up being criticised for its numerous bugs, awkward controls, and failing to meet the high expectations set by its promotional campaign.

976. **The Creative WaveBlaster** was an add-on MIDI daughterboard for Creative Sound Blaster 16 and AWE32 sound cards, intended to enhance the MIDI music playback quality in PC games and applications by providing higher quality instrument sounds, but it saw limited adoption due to the emerging dominance of software-based MIDI synthesis and digital audio.

977. **The ASUS VRM (Voltage Regulator Module) Daughterboard**, designed for some ASUS motherboards to provide additional voltage regulation for CPUs, allowing for better stability and overclocking. However, with evolving

motherboard designs that included more robust built-in voltage regulation, the need for such a daughterboard diminished.

JUICY CONTROVERSIES

978. **The Intel Pentium FDIV bug** in 1994 caused a massive controversy when it was discovered that Pentium processors could produce incorrect decimal results, leading to a public relations crisis and a costly recall for Intel.

979. **Microsoft's integration of Internet Explorer with Windows 95** led to antitrust lawsuits, alleging Microsoft used its operating system dominance to push out competitors like Netscape Navigator in the web browser market.

980. **IBM's DeathStar Hard Drives**, nicknamed due to their high failure rates, faced consumer backlash and class-action lawsuits, impacting IBM's reputation in the hard drive market.

981. **Apple's "Power Macintosh" series faced criticism** for its initial high prices and limited software availability, despite its innovative design and superior performance in certain applications.

982. **Creative's Sound Blaster 16 MultiCD issue**, where early versions of the card had compatibility issues with certain CD-ROM drives, frustrating users and requiring hardware revisions and driver updates.

983. **The controversy over the use of DRM (Digital Rights Management)** began to heat up in the late '90s as software and game publishers started to include more invasive DRM measures to combat piracy, leading to consumer backlash.

984. **3dfx Interactive's decision to prioritise retail graphics cards (Voodoo) over OEM sales** led to tensions with PC manufacturers and contributed to financial difficulties, eventually leading to the company's acquisition by NVIDIA.

Juicy Controversies

985. **The "DoubleClick privacy scandal" of 1999**, where the online ad company was found to be tracking users' internet habits without clear consent, raising early alarms over online privacy and leading to an FTC investigation.

986. **Rambus DRAM (RDRAM) controversy**, where Intel's push for the adoption of RDRAM in PCs due to its theoretically superior performance was met with high costs and compatibility issues, eventually leading to widespread industry support for the cheaper and more flexible DDR SDRAM.

987. **Cyrix vs. Intel legal battles** over CPU patents and the right to use certain x86 instructions, highlighting the fiercely competitive nature of the CPU market in the '90s.

988. **The "Leap Year Bug" (or "Y2K bug")**, while broader than just PCs, caused widespread concern that computers and software would fail en masse at the turn of the millennium due to the way dates were coded, leading to a massive, global effort to update and patch systems.

989. **Napster's rise in the late '90s** sparked a huge legal controversy over digital music piracy and copyright infringement, changing the music industry and how music was consumed.

990. **The initial public reception of the Java programming language by Sun Microsystems** was mixed, with some developers concerned about its performance compared to C++, though Java eventually became widely adopted for its "write once, run anywhere" capability.

991. **The controversy surrounding the "Clipper Chip"**, proposed by the U.S. government as a means of ensuring that all encrypted communication could be decrypted by authorities, raising early debates about encryption, privacy, and surveillance.

992. **The U.S. government's export restrictions on cryptographic software** in the 1990s, which limited

Juicy Controversies

encryption strength to 40 bits for software like web browsers exported out of the U.S., sparked controversy over national security vs. personal privacy. Companies like Netscape were forced to create weaker, export versions of their software, which were easily cracked by enthusiasts and researchers.

993. **The "CSS (Content Scramble System)" controversy**, where a program called DeCSS capable of decrypting DVD content was released in 1999, led to legal battles over copyright infringement vs. the right to circumvent DRM for fair use and compatibility purposes.

994. **Intel's CPU serial number controversy** in 1999, where the Pentium III processor was found to contain a unique serial number that could potentially be used to track users' activities online, leading to privacy concerns and backlash from consumers and privacy advocates.

995. **The First "Macro Virus", Melissa**, in 1999, marked a significant shift in computer security threats, demonstrating how easily viruses could spread through seemingly innocuous Word documents, leading to widespread alarm and a re-evaluation of email and internet security practices.

996. **Microsoft's "Windows Refund Day" protest in 1999**, where users dissatisfied with the Microsoft tax (the cost of Windows pre-installed on PCs) demanded refunds for the Windows OS they didn't intend to use, highlighting the issues around consumer choice and software licensing.

997. **The rise and fall of dot-com businesses** in the late '90s led to scepticism about the viability of internet companies, culminating in the dot-com bubble burst of 2000, which saw many high-profile startups and tech companies collapse, affecting the broader PC and technology market.

998. **The "BeOS" operating system**, developed by Be Inc., became a cult favourite for its multimedia capabilities and efficiency but faced an uphill battle for adoption due to

Microsoft's dominant position in the OS market, leading to controversies over anti-competitive practices.

999. **The failed merger between Compaq and Digital Equipment Corporation (DEC)** in 1998, intended to create a computing powerhouse, instead resulted in cultural clashes and strategic misalignments, contributing to Compaq's eventual acquisition by HP.

1000. **The controversy over "Web Standards" in the late '90s**, as web developers and users grappled with inconsistent browser implementations of HTML and CSS, leading to the formation of the Web Standards Project (WaSP) to advocate for consistent browser behaviour.

FINAL FACT

1001. **PGP (Pretty Good Privacy) encryption**, introduced in the early '90s as a ground breaking tool for securing electronic communications, was a beacon of hope for privacy advocates, symbolising the potential for individuals to protect their digital correspondence from prying eyes.

    Despite its early promise and continued use among a dedicated user base, the widespread adoption of email encryption has been hampered by usability challenges and the complexity of key management, leaving the majority of today's email traffic less secure than it could be, a reminder of the ongoing struggle between convenience and privacy in the digital age.

~

As we reach the end of this digital odyssey into the heart of 90s PC nostalgia, we hope this journey has rekindled old memories and maybe introduced you to some of the era's overlooked treasures. Now, we're eager to hear from you—what moments in this book struck a chord with your own nostalgic recollections? Which stories of technological triumphs and pixelated adventures resonated the most?

We invite you to share your favourite memories and thoughts in a review on Amazon. Your insights not only celebrate the legacy of 90s PC gaming but also guide fellow enthusiasts on their journey through this remarkable period in tech history.

If this book has ignited your curiosity or left you yearning for more discussions, we warmly welcome you to our community at **www.altara.media**. Engage in lively debates, share your unique perspectives, and stay abreast of our latest publications and exclusive announcements. Don't miss the chance to subscribe to our mailing list for updates straight to your inbox.

Join us in keeping the memories of 90s PC gaming alive and well.

Search for **altara.media** on social media.

Scan with your smartphone camera to review on Amazon.com

Visit www.altara.media.

Hear announcements!

View our books!

Sign up to our mailing list!

Join the discussion!

altara.media

Printed in Great Britain
by Amazon